What Narcissists DON'T Want You to Know

The Secrets of Understanding Narcissism and the Mindset of Toxic People

Elena Miro

© Copyright Elena Miro 2021 - All rights reserved.

The content contained within this book may not be reproduced, duplicated, or transmitted without direct written permission from the author or the publisher except for the use of brief quotations in a book review.

Under no circumstances will any blame or legal responsibility be held against the publisher, or author, for any damages, reparation, or monetary loss due to the information contained within this book. Either directly or indirectly. You are responsible for your own choices, actions, and results.

Legal Notice:

This book is copyright protected. This book is only for personal use. You cannot amend, distribute, sell, use, quote or paraphrase any part, or the content within this book, without the consent of the author or publisher except for the use of brief quotations in a book review.

Disclaimer notice:

Please note the information contained within this book is for educational and entertainment purposes only. All effort has been executed to present accurate, up to date, and reliable, complete information. No warranties of any kind are declared or implied. Readers acknowledge that the author is not engaging in the rendering of legal, financial, medical, or professional advice. The content within this book has been derived from various sources. Please consult a licensed professional before attempting any techniques outlined in this book.

By reading this book, the reader agrees that under no circumstances is the author responsible for any losses, direct or indirect, which are incurred as a result of the use of the information contained within this book, including, but not limited to,—errors, omissions, or inaccuracies.

From the Author **9**

Introduction **13**

Chapter One: What is Narcissism? **20**

    Real-Life Experiences with Narcissism   20
    What is this Confusing Condition?   22
    Formal Definition and Traits of Narcissism   23
    Personality Disorders   29
    Diagnosing and Treating Personality Disorders   33
    Treatment 36
    Conclusion 38

Chapter Two: Is Everyone a Narcissist? **40**

    Tales from the Trenches   40
    Narcissism and Culture   43
    Can a Narcissist Change Their Spots? 49
    Learned Responses 51
    Conclusion 53

Chapter Three: Understanding the Different Kinds of Narcissism **55**

    A Little History   56
    Healthy Forms of Narcissism 57
    Unhealthy Forms of Narcissism   59
    Antisocial Narcissism   62
    Prosocial Narcissism   63
    Malignant Narcissism   64
    Grandiose Narcissism   65
    Vulnerable (or Covert) Narcissism   66
    A Rose by Any Other Name…   67

Yet Another Model 69
Conclusion 72

Chapter Four: The Modern Era of Narcissism, Entitlement, and Toxic People *73*

Public Comments about Cultural Narcissism   74
The Science of Narcissistic Cultures   76
Cultural Features that Encourage Narcissism   81
Corporate Capitalism and Narcissism 87
Conclusion 91

Chapter Five: How Narcissism Develops to Create a Toxic Person *93*

How is NPD Diagnosed?   94
How Does NPD Develop?   97
What's Happening Internally?   103
A Few Insights from the Trenches   105
Conclusion 107

Chapter Six: How Do You Know They're a Narcissist? 108

Stories from the Veterans of Narcissism   109
Trends Indicating Narcissism 114
They Seem Likable at First   116
When the Change Happens   117
Less Obvious Traits of Narcissism   122
Conclusion 128

Chapter Seven: From Charm to Harm—How a Psychopathic Narcissist Thinks and Feels 129

Inside the Mind of a Narcissist   130
Toxic Thoughts   135
Who is the Inner Critic?   137

Are They Really Insecure, or Do They Believe the Inner Hype?   140
Narcissistic Behaviors—"Manipulationships"   143
Trauma Bonding   149
Can a Narcissist Break Free of the Pattern?   151
Conclusion 154

Chapter Eight: What Narcissists Fear the Most and Why They are Like That   *155*

From the Trenches... 156
What Do the Experts Say?   159
Conclusion 169

Chapter Nine: Empaths, Success Stories, and Other Types that Attract Narcissists   *170*

Why Do I Attract Narcissists?   171
What Do the Experts Say?   175
Conclusion 183

Chapter Ten: Can an Egotistical Toxic Person Truly Love You?   *185*

From the Trenches…   187
How Do Narcissists Love?   191
Narcissistic Love   194
How is Love Measured?   197
Conclusion 199

Final Words 201

From the Author

Dear Reader,

You hear a lot about narcissism these days. Narcissists seem to be everywhere and in every part of life. We used to think of them as toxic people, someone you should avoid at all costs. They were disrespected, judged, and even hated, but do we really understand this condition? Do we really know who they are?

I survived narcissistic abuse from a spouse, so I know what you might be going through if you're dealing with a toxic person. I understand the pain, misunderstanding, and confusion. I share your tears, and I have suffered through those sleepless, anxious nights. This experience motivated me to do my own in-depth research into this mental condition. In fact, I went on to get a degree in psychology, write books on the subject, and speak to hundreds of my readers and patients about what they're going through.

I found myself discussing the topic of modern narcissism with colleagues, friends, and many of you, my readers. I soon realized that so many people living with a narcissist or other toxic person in their life don't have the same choice I did. They are unable to leave like I was able to. Many of them share children with a narcissistic spouse. Some have narcissistic children they refuse to leave behind. Lots of people work with a narcissist, and they can't leave their job. Some of you just quite simply still love the narcissist in your life and don't want to leave.

I can't help everyone with a toxic person in their life, but I can share my experiences and knowledge that I have gained to help those of you who can't or don't want to leave your narcissistic abuser. I want to help you understand these monsters, so you can develop compassion for their state of mind. In fact, you'll hear firsthand from narcissists what they're thinking and feeling. You'll gain valuable insight into toxic people and the truth that is hiding behind their emotionally abusive behavior.

Believe it or not, living happily with a narcissist is possible, and you can even turn that person into someone who is more loving and easier to deal with. To do that, you must first understand the mental condition they are struggling with and how you can better manage your interactions with them, so they will stay positive and free of the typical manipulative behavior that narcissists often exhibit.

This first book in this set of two will be dedicated to gaining a better understanding of narcissism and how it develops. You'll gain valuable insight into how the narcissist thinks and how that affects their behavior. You'll also have a better understanding of the kind of people that attract narcissists and why, as well as whether the narcissist can truly love you or not.

The second book in the series will present proven strategies for dealing with the toxic person in your life. You'll learn how to avoid being codependent, how to set strong boundaries, and how to manage your interactions properly with this difficult person. You can make choices that will help you live a happy, fulfilling life, and you might even help them heal along the way.

What's more—and what I feel is valuable and unique about these books—is that you will hear from real people who have been dealing with real narcissists in their lives. These stories come from my friends, readers, colleagues, patients, and various social media sites like Facebook and Quora. Like you, they were simply unable—for many reasons—to leave that person behind, and they had to find a way to exist with them peacefully. What they have learned can help you too.

These books will bring together advice from people living with narcissists, professional psychologists, published studies, and even narcissists themselves that can help you create a happy life with the toxic person you love.

I know what it's like to live with a narcissist because I was married to one. I thought he was the perfect man for me, but after it was too late, I learned he was toxic. My experiences with him caused me to want to reach out to others who might be suffering like I was. I want to help you with what I have learned, particularly if you have made the decision to stay with your narcissist. That's what these books are all about, and it is my sincere wish that they help you create a better life for yourself.

Introduction

> People have a habit of inventing fictions they will believe wholeheartedly in order to ignore the truth they cannot accept.

If you have a narcissist in your life in any capacity, you've likely been advised to run away from that person as fast as you can. It's not bad advice, but it's also not always possible. What if the narcissist was your boss or coworker? What if your child was a narcissist? What if your husband was toxic, but you still loved him and didn't want to leave or are financially dependent on him and can't leave?

There are many reasons why you might choose to stay in a toxic relationship with a narcissist, but while there are many books out there that will advise you to get away, very few talk about what to do to make a relationship with a narcissist actually work. That is, until now.

This book is the first of a set that focuses on understanding narcissism and toxic people and learning how to live with them happily. That's right, I mean happily—not just surviving, but actually thriving. If you must stay in a relationship with a psychopath, then you have to learn all about their condition and how to protect yourself. What better way to do that than to hear from people who are living with a narcissist, professionals who study and treat narcissistic personality disorder (NPD), and even narcissists themselves?

In this book, you'll hear the experiences and opinions of hundreds of real people who needed to find a way to survive living with a toxic person in their life. They will share their firsthand experience with narcissism, whether from the view of someone suffering from narcissistic abuse, their abuser, or their therapist. Though the names have been changed to protect their privacy, you will hear about their real experiences and what they did to survive and thrive.

You'll learn about how narcissists think from actual narcissists. You'll hear the advice from people who have successfully been living with them for years, and you'll hear from the psychological professionals who have devoted their careers to understanding them. You'll come away with a better understanding of narcissistic personality disorder, and you'll also learn how to protect your own mental and physical health from toxic people.

You deserve to have a happy life, even if you can never help them have one. These books will give you the information and advice you need to understand the situation and learn how to interact with your narcissist in a way that lets you lead a fulfilling, satisfying, and yes, happy life.

I know what it's like to live with a narcissistic psychopath. I was married to one, and I made the decision to leave. But I was so affected by the situation that I decided to get a degree in psychology and devote my career to helping people deal with this frustrating and sometimes dangerous mental health condition. You can read about my story in my first book, *My Toxic Husband: Loving and Breaking Up with a Narcissistic Man—Start Your Psychopath-free Life Now!*

In that book, you'll hear about my experience of meeting someone whom I thought was the perfect man for me, but who turned out to be a psychopathic narcissist. I was left confused and devastated by the sudden change in his behavior, I so I left him. It was the best decision for me since we didn't have children together or share real estate, and I had my own place and savings.

It took me a while to recover from the emotional abuse I had suffered. I knew nothing about narcissism, but I was determined to learn more. After recovering, I realized I wanted to help other women in the same situation. I learned all about this mental condition, got my degree in psychology, and started writing so I could help others in similar situations. That's why I wrote my second book—*FREE YOURSELF! A Complex PTSD Recovery Workbook for Women: 10 Steps to Go from Emotional Abuse Recovery to Building Healthy Relationships*—to help those women who have made the decision to leave their toxic husbands. I wanted to provide them with a road map to recovery.

In that book, I wrote about narcissistic victim syndrome and how someone who has suffered this kind of emotional abuse can recover. Because this syndrome keeps you from seeing the truth and making the best decisions for yourself and your family, I created a special therapeutic program that is included in this book to help women see their situations more clearly. It comes with a recovery workbook as well, which will help you get out of the fog that is keeping you from seeing what's going on and recover from the abuse you suffered. It also helps you develop better coping strategies, so you will never suffer in an emotionally abusive relationship again.

Recovery can be a difficult and slow process, and it took some time, but I also realized along the way that I was able and wanted to leave. I was lucky in the sense that I had a choice, but what about other people who either can't or don't want to leave their emotionally abusive relationships? That's why I decided to write this book, as well as the second one in this set, to help people who have made the decision to stay in a relationship with a narcissist. It can be done successfully.

Surprisingly, there are many people who have lived happily for years with toxic spouses, children, parents, bosses, coworkers, and friends. How have they done it? Well, they began by learning all about the mental condition that affects the toxic person in their life. That's what you can do now by reading this book.

You'll learn about what is meant by narcissism and narcissistic personality disorder, as well as how the modern era promotes that kind of mentality. You'll come to understand how narcissists think, along with what scares them. You'll also have a better understanding of why you might just be what a psychopathic narcissist is looking for, and you'll discover whether they can truly ever love you or not.

If there's ever going to be a chance for you to make it work with the narcissist in your life, you first have to understand the condition. Only then can you take the steps you need to take to protect yourself from their toxicity and manipulations. Once you know how to protect yourself, you can create a satisfying relationship with them on your terms. The second book in this set will cover how to do that, but let's start with understanding.

With understanding comes compassion, and that will empower you to set the parameters you will accept for a healthy relationship—one that will allow you to live a satisfying life. Although this book is not a panacea, and there is no guarantee that it will save your relationship with a narcissist, knowledge will give you power, and with that power, you can work to at least improve your relationship. It's almost impossible to change or cure a narcissist, but there are ways to work toward a satisfying relationship with them. Let's begin this journey with new hope for the future—one where you can find the satisfaction and love you seek, even with a narcissist in your life.

Chapter One: **What is Narcissism?**

"How starved you must have been that my heart became a meal for your ego." —Amanda Torroni

Before we get into the technical explanations and definitions, it's helpful to hear a few of the real-life experiences people have had with this mental condition.

Real-Life Experiences with Narcissism

Bill, a self-identified narcissist, describes what it feels like as he interacts with other people. He says he's aware that he's acting like an "asshole," but he truly believes that it's the fault of those around him that he must act that way. They deserve it in his mind. He also knows that deep down, he experiences a sense of self-loathing, but he dares not face that issue head-on. He prefers his delusions over reality. For him, it's a form of escapism, whereby he can just say, "fuck reality, fuck facts!" He says, "I have to get my needs met. I ***deserve*** to get my needs met."

Carol, who's lived with a narcissist for many years, describes him as being delusional in his belief that he's perfect and always in the right. She says he feels justified in his need to control everything and everyone because he knows he is right, and he is pervasive in his sense of entitlement. He truly believes that the world owes him. He devalues everyone else and overvalues himself. Nothing, she notes, compares to his ego.

Jay describes his experience with his narcissistic wife as one where she simply goes off into "la-la land" at a moment's notice. He says they'll be talking about some subject, and suddenly, she'll start ranting about something offensive he had done that has little relation to the subject at hand. He finds himself on the defensive with no understanding of how the conversation transitioned to this topic. It leaves him feeling confused, attacked, and shamed. Moreover, it takes him hours to get her back to the original topic, which is usually something important they need to resolve.

What is this Confusing Condition?

As you can see from the real-life descriptions above, narcissism is a confusing and frustrating mental condition. But before we can really understand the narcissist, we have to know what narcissism is, and perhaps equally as importantly, what it is not. Is someone who is vain a narcissist? Is someone who thinks they are better than other people a narcissist? As we see in the testimonials above, those are narcissistic traits, but that doesn't mean those people are narcissists. It's become fashionable to refer to anyone who seems like a bad person as a narcissist, but are they really? So, just what constitutes narcissism?

If you have healthy self-esteem, you will have some narcissistic traits. Narcissism, like other mental conditions, exists on a continuum. There are degrees of narcissistic traits, and to be diagnosed with narcissistic personality disorder (NPD), you have to have several traits that are a predominant part of your personality. Having a few of those traits isn't enough, but before we go any further, let's examine the official definition of narcissism and the toxic traits associated with the condition.

Formal Definition and Traits of Narcissism

The fifth edition of the American Psychiatric Association's *Diagnostic and Statistical Manual of Mental Disorders (DSM-5)* defines NPD as "comprising a pervasive pattern of grandiosity (in fantasy or behavior), a constant need for admiration, and a lack of empathy, beginning by early adulthood and present in a variety of contexts, as indicated by the presence of at least 5 of the following 9 criteria" (Ambardar, 2019):

1. A grandiose sense of self-importance;
2. A preoccupation with fantasies of unlimited success, power, brilliance, beauty, or ideal love;
3. A belief that he or she is special and unique and can only be understood by, or should associate with, other special or high-status people or institutions;
4. A need for excessive admiration;
5. A sense of entitlement;
6. Interpersonally exploitive behavior;
7. A lack of empathy;
8. Envy of others or a belief that others are envious of him or her;
9. A demonstration of arrogant and haughty behaviors or attitudes.

To be diagnosed with NPD, a person must demonstrate several characteristics over an extended period of time. These traits point to how the narcissist has an inflated sense of their own importance, which thus manifests as a deep need for admiration and adoration. This is combined with a lack of empathy for other people, and as you already know, that can result in troubled relationships.

The thing is that, although they have this inflated sense of importance, underneath that lies a very fragile self-esteem that makes the narcissist vulnerable to any kind of criticism. This combination of an exaggerated sense of importance combined with a fragile ego manifests in the following symptoms.

- They have a sense of entitlement—they believe themselves to be deserving of special treatment because of their inflated sense of importance;
- They require excessive admiration, validation, and adoration—if you're not focused on their every need, they feel slighted;
- They believe themselves to be superior, regardless of their achievements or lack thereof, and they expect to be recognized as such;
- Because they believe themselves to be superior, they will often exaggerate their talents and achievements;

- They believe they can only associate with people who are also special, but they will never recognize them as being as special as they are. They will also try to "take down" people they believe are better, as that will show just how special they are;
- They will usually monopolize conversations, and if they believe you to be inferior to them (which they do for almost everyone), they will belittle or look down on you;
- They expect to be given special favors;
- They demand unquestioned compliance with their wishes;
- They will not hesitate to take advantage of other people to achieve their goals;
- They won't recognize the needs or feelings of other people because they can't;
- They are arrogant and often behave in a haughty manner, which manifests as being boastful, pretentious, and conceited;
- They insist on only the best, whether it's their car, office, or home, because they believe they deserve nothing less.

> You will never get the truth out of a Narcissist. The closest you will ever come is a story that either makes them the victim or the hero, but never the villian.
>
> Shannon L. Alder

When they are confronted with even the slightest criticism, they feel extremely threatened and will frequently react in one of the following ways:

- If they believe they are not being treated in a special enough way, they may become very impatient and even angry. For example, they might snap at a waiter who doesn't seem to be giving them the devoted attention they believe they should receive. Jennifer described the nightmare of going out to eat with her toxic husband, *"Once he had decided the waiter was no good, he loudly criticized his every move. It was mortifying"*;
- They are easily offended and may respond with rage or contempt to even the gentlest suggestion. Jim, a narcissist, reveals that he feels the same kind of threat when criticized—no matter how gentle the critique—as if his very life is being threatened. He feels an immediate need to respond and an almost

uncontrollable urge to "crush" the person criticizing him;
- They often belittle other people to make themselves feel and appear superior. Jonathan notes that his narcissistic wife frequently tells their friends how inept he is at handyman tasks. She often tells stories about how she has to fix an appliance or redo a home improvement project after he did it. He describes feeling emasculated by her demeaning treatment of him;
- They are unable to appropriately regulate their emotions and behavior. Another narcissist, Trevor, describes that he simply can't control his rage. When he is triggered, it's as if a bomb explodes inside him, and he can't stop himself from yelling and belittling the person responsible. The context does little to quell his rage. He will yell at a coworker in front of others as readily as he will his wife in the privacy of their home;
- They have great difficulty dealing with any stress, and they struggle with adapting to change. Carol describes her narcissistic husband Mark as a virtual slave to his routine. He experiences great stress if anything causes a change to his normal pattern, and he often blames her if that happens;

- They may become depressed if they feel they are falling short of perfection. Jon expresses a great sense of failure over even the smallest problem that he can't resolve quickly. He notes, *"I feel like I'm a loser if something I'm doing—even if it's the first time I've tried it—doesn't work out";*
- They harbor secret feelings of shame, vulnerability, insecurity, and humiliation. Steven describes his almost constant fear of being exposed as a fraud. He has worked hard to get where he is in his job, but he still believes that someday, someone will come along and expose him as a fake.

These descriptions give you some insight into what the narcissist is thinking and how their symptoms cause problems in their life. It's no wonder that narcissists typically have problems with forming and maintaining relationships, be they romantic, professional, familial, or even just friendships. This usually means they end up unhappy and disappointed with their lives, particularly since it seems like they are not getting the admiration, special treatment, or favors they believe they deserve.

Many people think of narcissism as being excessively vain, but according to psychologist Dr. Ramani Durvasula, although taking and posting selfies and checking your look in the mirror every chance you get are narcissistic tendencies, the fact that you have those tendencies doesn't necessarily mean you're a narcissist.

In fact, she believes that narcissism has been badly misunderstood. It's become a bit of a buzz word in our modern society. Dr. Durvasula identifies four main pillars of narcissism. These are a lack of empathy, a chronic sense of entitlement, grandiosity, and a desperate need to seek out validation and admiration. These pillars are the core of the personality disorder.

Personality Disorders

Narcissism is what is characterized as a Cluster B personality disorder, but what does it mean to have a personality disorder, and what is Cluster B? Let's start with what characterizes a personality disorder.

A personality disorder is a mental condition whereby you think in a very rigid, unhealthy pattern that also results in unhealthy behaviors. People who have personality disorders typically have problems relating to other people and situations. This results in social problems that can affect both their personal and professional lives.

Because someone like a narcissist has likely been that way most—if not all—of their life, they often don't even know they have a problem. It just seems natural to them. When they face challenges, they don't realize that part of the problem lies with their own behavior, and so they tend to blame other people around them.

Most personality disorders begin when you're young, during your teenage years, or in early adulthood. There are different kinds of personality disorders which are categorized in clusters. Disorders in each cluster show similar signs and symptoms. It is also true that many people who have one personality disorder may also have a second one as well.

- **Cluster A Personality Disorders**

    These disorders all are characterized by eccentric, odd thinking and/or behavior. They include conditions such as paranoid personality disorder and schizoid personality disorder.

- **Cluster B Personality Disorders**

  This is the category that includes narcissistic personality disorder, and all of the disorders in this cluster are characterized by dramatic, unpredictable, or overly emotional behaviors and thinking. Aside from NPD, this cluster also includes borderline personality disorder, antisocial personality disorder, and histrionic personality disorder.

- **Cluster C Personality Disorders**

  The disorders in this cluster are characterized by anxious, fearful thinking and behaviors. Examples include avoidant personality disorder and obsessive-compulsive personality disorder.

Diagnosing and Treating Personality Disorders

Personality disorders aren't new, but they were first really described around the beginning of the 20th century as part of Freudian analysis. During that time, psychologists and psychiatrists were first describing a variety of personality differences that they were seeing in patients.

Although certain symptoms of mental disorders were readily identifiable, others were less clear. Personality disorders fall into that category because they are, in a sense, intrinsic to the individual. They are woven into the fabric of their personality. It makes it hard to know you have a problem because it just seems normal, and it makes it just as hard for a therapist to spot.

That doesn't mean that people are always blind to what's going on. Even the most defended narcissist can sometimes see their own blind spots and weaknesses. But usually, they have to *want* to understand why they have certain challenges in their life, and for many people with NPD, they often have trouble seeing themselves as the source of any problem.

As for the professionals who are trying to study and treat these kinds of disorders, it can also be hard to identify the specific problem. As the science reporter for the New York Times, Benedict Carey, notes, professionals need training beyond the usual education they get to spot these problems as well.

Another reason this is so problematic to identify is that people who suffer from something like narcissistic personality disorder can also have other symptoms like depression and anxiety. Those are easier to spot and tend to get treated, whereas the underlying condition ends up going undiagnosed. What's more, even experts disagree on the specifics of each disorder.

Another problem that was pointed out by Dr. Pat Webster, clinical psychologist and author of the book *Winning at Love: The Alpha Male's Guide to Relationship Success,* is that certain disorders like NPD are endemic. She argues that the US has become a "culture of narcissists." Because of that, the traits associated with NPD often get rewarded in that context.

Moreover, there are a lot of people running around with personality disorders. Dr. Mark Lenzenweger, a psychology professor at Binghamton University, notes that approximately one in every ten Americans suffers from some kind of diagnosable personality disorder (NPR Talk of the Nation, 2012). Now, that's not all NPD. The prevalence of NPD is estimated at approximately 0.5 percent of the general population of the United States. Interestingly, it was found in 20 percent of the military population and 17 percent of the population of first-year medical students (Sheenie Ambardar & Bienenfeld, 2019). That might reflect the success accorded certain symptoms in people who have NPD.

According to Lenzenweger, diagnosing a patient with a personality disorder involves a complicated process of sifting through their life history in order to ensure the symptoms are long-standing—i.e., have gone on for at least five years—and then separating out transitory symptoms like anxiety and depression, which can complicate the diagnosis. Only after this due diligence can the professional be certain they're dealing with a personality disorder. Oftentimes, clinicians and patients alike don't have that kind of time, and that's certainly true for the loved ones who are trying to deal with the narcissist at home. Finally, to be diagnosed, the person suffering from NPD has to actually seek out treatment, and because they aren't really aware or admit that they have a problem, this rarely happens.

Treatment

If a narcissist does seek out help, the treatment they receive will vary in accordance with a number of factors. The main treatment is talk therapy, also known as psychotherapy, but the patient might also be given certain medications, particularly if they have other mental health conditions like depression.

With psychotherapy, the goal is to help the narcissist relate better to other people, so they can form and maintain more intimate and rewarding relationships. It is also designed to help them understand the causes of their emotions, why they feel the need to compete with other people, why they can't trust others, and ultimately to get at the self-loathing that's driving the behavior.

With time, a narcissist can learn to accept responsibility for their actions and maintain good personal relationships, successfully collaborate with coworkers, recognize their own abilities, tolerate criticism, learn from failure, regulate their emotions, build self-esteem, and let go of what they cannot control. They can also learn better coping strategies for times of stress. The support of their family and friends is a necessary element of successful treatment.

There exist no medications approved specifically for treating NPD, but clinicians will often prescribe medication for symptoms that accompany the disorder, like anxiety. There are, however, some lifestyle changes that can be implemented to help alleviate the worst of the symptoms. These include things like keeping an open mind and remembering what the goal of treatment is, sticking to the plan by attending your scheduled therapy sessions, and taking any prescribed medications as directed. They should also treat other problems like alcohol or drug abuse, as well as mental health problems, and engage in family therapy to learn new strategies for interacting with loved ones.

Conclusion

In sum, you can see how complex narcissistic personality disorder is, and it's no wonder that so many people continue to suffer without any real treatment. Most of the time, they don't even realize, or won't admit, that they have a problem. Even if they do, getting a correct diagnosis can be a challenge, and then there's the problem of sticking to a treatment regimen, something many narcissists simply won't do.

That paints a rather bleak picture for the loved ones of the narcissist, but all is not lost. There are ways that you can take control over the kind of treatment you will permit, and this can help you shape the behavior of your narcissistic loved one. We'll discuss this more in the second book in this set, but for now, let's talk about whether narcissism is actually endemic in the United States or any culture.

Chapter Two: Is Everyone a Narcissist?

"When the healthy pursuit of self-interest and self-realization turns into self-absorption, other people can lose their intrinsic value in our eyes and become mere means to the fulfillment of our needs and desires." — P.M. Forni

As in the previous chapter—and in each chapter going forward—we'll begin with a few stories from the real experts on this topic, which are the people living with narcissists and the narcissists themselves.

Tales from the Trenches

Sharon had just ended her fourth relationship with a narcissist. She struggled to understand why she seemed to find so many toxic people. She often asked herself, *"Why are they attracted to me?"* Another time, she lamented in a social media post, *"Did you notice that most relationships you have in your life have been lies? Toxic, malevolent sadists seem to be everywhere!"*

From peers and professionals alike, we see a variety of answers to her statement. Marilyn responds by noting that narcissism has become a sensational news topic, given that it is seen among our "highest leaders." She states it might also be a generational problem but notes that it is among the most underreported mental conditions. Additionally, narcissists typically have larger numbers of relationships simply because of the cycle of "idealization, devaluation, and discard" in which they engage. For that reason, one narcissist can effectively do a lot of damage to many people. Finally, she offers up the idea that narcissism can thrive in secrecy when families don't want to admit there's a problem.

Other respondents like Wayne point to an article posted on the Association for Psychological Science website that cites two psychologists who argued that culture was to blame. In the United States, much of the media focuses on personal image, and that combined with a rapid rise in social media fosters the concept that "it's all about me."

But, others disagree. One respondent posted that there are not more narcissists, and he claims to have over 40 years of "invested study." He argues that culture does play a role, in the sense that certain words are thrown around until they lose all meaning. In other words, maybe we're just calling more people narcissists because they do something we don't like. Furthermore, he states that we don't have to label every kind of human behavior as a mental disorder, but we get in the habit of tossing around labels like "narcissist" far too easily. Sometimes, people just get irritated and act out in a selfish or senseless way, but that doesn't mean they are narcissists. In fact, our culture has become somewhat of a victim culture where everyone wants to lay claim to being someone else's "victim." That way, they don't have to take responsibility for their own behavior.

Kate, who has a Masters degree in psychology, notes that narcissism exists on a spectrum and that having some is healthy. You need to have some confidence in yourself to take action and risk failure. That's the only way to make things happen. But you need to have some empathy, honest self-awareness, and an awareness of others to temper that sense of self. Without that, your focus can become so narrow that your narcissistic tendencies become pathological.

So, who's right? Are there more narcissists for cultural—or other—reasons, or has everyone simply been overusing the term? Are there toxic, malevolent sadists everywhere, or are we just afraid there are? Can we even know the truth?

Narcissism and Culture

Campbell and Twenge (2013) in an article posted on the Association for Psychological Science website examined the relationship between cultural values and narcissism. They pose the question, "Can an entire culture be narcissistic?" They then go on to argue that it is possible, and it seems to be a major trend in the United States.

Cultural narcissism is a concept that has been around since the late 1970s. It was described extensively in the book, *The Culture of Narcissism*, which was published in 1979. In that book, cultural historian Christopher Lasch argued that cultural narcissism is something we see reflected in our TV shows, song lyrics, and cultural trends toward vanity, entitlement, materialism, and the constant search for fame.

Campbell and Twenge (2013) argue that there are documented increases in those cultural factors and that although those changes in cultural values are larger than the increase in individual narcissism, they promote individual narcissistic behavior. In fact, they encourage and applaud behaviors that used to be seen as morally unacceptable in US culture. For example, these cultural trends encourage individuals to embrace life goals that center on money, fame and maintaining a certain image. That fact, the researchers argue, has resulted in an increase in narcissism among individuals.

Campbell and Twenge (2013) pointed to studies that indicate young Americans are three times more likely than people over the age of 60 to have experienced narcissistic personality disorder in their lifetime. There is also research that examines self-reported traits related to narcissism and shows that younger generations are more likely to have various narcissistic characteristics. For example, they have less empathy, see themselves as being above average with regard to leadership abilities and the necessary drive to achieve, frequently set unrealistically high goals, and tend to report higher levels of self-esteem. In short, they have no qualms focusing on themselves and showing off what they believe to be their best traits, even if those traits don't exactly jive with reality. This trend of "showing off" is something that is becoming far more common in our culture.

Perhaps the focus on self began as people started to set themselves apart from the crowd through their offspring. Campbell and Twenge (2013) noted that the names people give their children are becoming more unique. During the 1940s, about 30 percent of boys had one of the top ten most popular names of the time, but by 2010, that number has shrunk to only one in nine—or only about 10 percent. That is coupled with a decline in the use of plural pronouns like we, us, and our, and an increase in the use of singular pronouns like I, me, and mine in books on Google and lyrics of top 10 songs.

There is also other data that shows an increase in focus on the individual and their image. Since the 1990s, there has been a significant increase in medical cosmetic procedures to maintain a certain look, houses have more rooms devoted to individual activities rather than family fun, and religion has become more devoted to personal endeavors like individual prosperity and direct experiences with the divine (Campbell and Twenge, 2013).

Everything seems to be focusing more on the self and less on the community or group. You can get your personalized meal from any restaurant, and you can order it on your iPhone. You don't even have to be bothered to interact with the wait staff. It's all designed to set up what can easily develop into a sense of entitlement. In a sense, it provides the individual with an idea of freedom that carries no responsibility, tells them they can have a relationship without any personal sacrifice, and it encourages them to develop positive self-views without having to ground those in reality. You might like to think you have the powers of Superman, but if you jump off a building to try and fly, you will experience the reality of being grounded very quickly. But, many young people have never been turned down for anything they want, told they can't do or have something, nor had to think of what other people might want or need.

What's more is that in our current reality, there are ever increasing opportunities in social realms to be less constrained by reality, such as in online social media forums. There, people can engage in virtual realities where they can, in fact, fly. They can participate in fantasy roleplaying and other online social realities where their narcissistic self-image is nourished. That's one possibility, but psychologist Pat MacDonald argues that there are other ways to deal with the epidemic of narcissism as well.

MacDonald (2014) agrees that there is an epidemic of narcissistic traits although NPD itself remains a rare clinical diagnosis. In many cultures around the world, there has been an increase in levels of greed, arrogance, self-obsession, superficial relationships, and vanity, and those trends are being promoted by social media with its focus on "everything me all the time." Furthermore, the interconnectedness fostered by our technology makes it difficult to escape these trends. We see wide-scale corruption that results from group greed and grandiosity—perhaps best illustrated in the banking realm—and that has led to increasing distrust in organizations. Because we are so focused on our own individual needs, we can't even bring ourselves to act to protect the very environment that nourishes us and the species with which we share the planet.

We'll take an in-depth look at these cultural phenomena in a later chapter, but from this brief foundation, it's no wonder that professionals are seeing a rise in clients who score higher on the narcissistic spectrum (MacDonald, 2014). Can it be changed, or are we doomed? Is there a way to understand what is going on better and work to ground people in a shared sense of reality, empathy, compassion, and kindness? Can people become less narcissistic?

Can a Narcissist Change Their Spots?

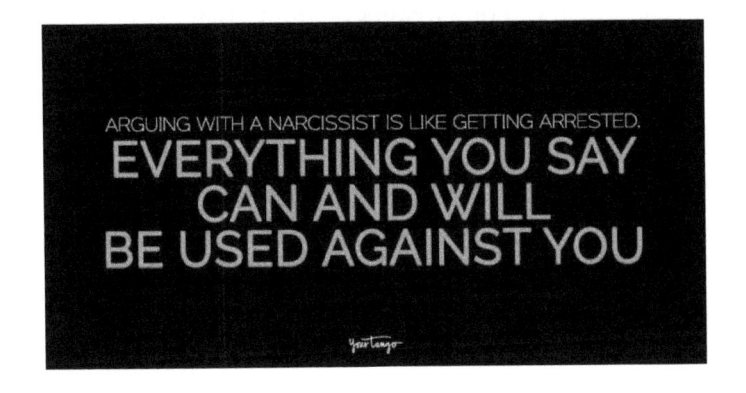

> ARGUING WITH A NARCISSIST IS LIKE GETTING ARRESTED.
> **EVERYTHING YOU SAY CAN AND WILL BE USED AGAINST YOU**

Most people will tell you that narcissists won't change, in part because they don't truly believe they are the cause of the problem and are also simply too frightened to face the demons that cause their worst behavior. There is some truth to that, but in reality, there are people who have NPD who *do* want to change. Many sufferers from this disorder will seek out and stay in therapy.

Therapy is not easy for a narcissist because they find it extremely difficult to admit they have any flaws. If they do that, they have to then deal with the shame they feel deep down almost constantly. It's also very difficult for anyone to do the difficult work of confronting one's demons in order to find healthier ways of functioning and coping with life's challenges.

Psychotherapists also find it difficult to work with narcissists since they are often the target of their rage. Psychologist Elinor Greenberg notes that narcissists have one of several possible responses in therapy. They are either idealizing their therapist, acting nicer than they really are, or devaluing the psychologist, as is typical for them to do to many people in their lives. They will frequently yell at their psychologist whenever they are triggered, something the therapy is designed to do in order to help them learn to cope in a healthier way (Greenberg, 2018).

Still, when the narcissist and therapist are both able to stick it out, it is well worth the effort. With the proper help, they can find a better way to live and interact with the people they love. Many of them do realize they are acting inappropriately when they get angry, but they don't know why that happens or how to stop it.

They also feel how radically their self-esteem fluctuates and can get tired of having to chase down new sources of validation constantly. They typically look for that outside validation, but they soon realize that nothing seems to be making a difference in their life—not the new dating interest, better job, or new toy in their life. No matter what they do, they still sink into those self-loathing and shame-based depressions that leave them feeling helpless against their own harsh self-criticism.

Although they might never admit it to you, they want to find a better way; they just don't know how. Moreover, the way they treat their loved ones drives them away, so it's hard to generate sympathetic responses when they do reach out for help. So, what can they do?

Learned Responses

Put simply, you can think of NPD as simply an adaptation to an early childhood environment that left the narcissist feeling like no one was empathizing with them. It was an environment in which they were not supported or applauded, and thus, their self-esteem is very unstable. To survive in that environment, the child did what any child does: they developed a particular set of coping skills that worked for them, and those have since become automatic. Really, the narcissist's responses when triggered are little more than habits.

The thing about a habit is that it becomes encoded in your brain. There are actually specialized neurons that will trigger the running of a habit routine in response to a cue. Once the routine is run, the brain is rewarded with a shot of dopamine—the brain's own feel-good neurochemical—which boosts your mood.

For example, when you hear your alarm in the morning, that is a trigger that cues a habit routine. Perhaps the routine is to get out of bed and make coffee. Each time you repeat the habit routine, certain pathways in your brain are reinforced. That's what makes the routine automatic: so that you don't really have to think about what you're doing. You rise out of bed, walk zombie-like to where the coffee machine is located, load it up, and push the button to make your coffee, all without thinking about it. You might even be thinking about something entirely different while you're doing this.

Normally, creating habit routines with specialized neurons for starting, running, and stopping the routine is helpful so your mind can focus on other things. But, when we're talking about a habit, those reinforced pathways make that well-ingrained habit routine difficult to quit. Difficult, but not impossible. You can choose to learn new habits and coping skills. That's essentially what a narcissist needs to do.

Just like the habit routine of making coffee when the alarm goes off, narcissistic responses to triggers are encoded in their brain. With practice, even the most hardened narcissist can learn new non-narcissistic and healthier strategies for responding to triggers. They can simply replace their old responses with new, better ones. It's kind of like updating an app, only instead of their telephone, they update their narcissistic behaviors with new strategies.

Conclusion

In sum, the answer posed by the chapter title is no—not everyone is a narcissist, but everyone does have some narcissistic traits, even people who are healthy. Narcissism becomes a problem when a person displays more than five of the traits listed in the DSM consistently for a long period of time. Anyone can be a little selfish, a little arrogant, or a little out of sorts every once in a while. It's when that becomes your habitual way of responding that you might have NPD.

Are there cultural elements that are leading to an epidemic of narcissistic behavior? Well, possibly. Many experts point to certain cultural values that reward narcissistic behavior, but that doesn't mean we're doomed to becoming a narcissistic culture. We can make better choices, just as individual narcissists can make better choices. We'll explore those topics more in Chapter Four, but suffice it to say that narcissism is a combination of learned responses, and therefore, it can be unlearned. Before we go any further into that discussion, let's discuss the different kinds of narcissists.

Chapter Three: **Understanding the Different Kinds of Narcissism**

"Narcissists are consumed with maintaining a shallow false self to others. They're emotionally crippled souls that are addicted to attention. Because of this they use a multitude of games, in order to receive adoration." —Shannon L. Alder

You might not realize this, but there are actually different kinds of narcissism, but this topic is not without controversy. Let's explore just how many kinds of narcissists there are and how their behavior differs.

A Little History

Sigmund Freud first argued that all humans pass through what he referred to as a developmental stage known as "primary narcissism", coined in 1914. Freud defined this developmental stage as one where the infant is in a self-centered frame of mind and can't cognitively understand that other people are separate entities. Freud claimed that this was simply a normal, healthy stage of development that all humans pass through. However, he also realized that it was possible to exaggerate that healthy narcissism and carry it into one's adult personality.

It was Karen Horney, another psychologist, who wrote that particular parenting styles could result in unhealthy adult narcissism in the 1940s. Specifically, she noted that parents who either overvalue or undervalue their children are creating an environment in which those children might grow up with an excessive need for praise and validation from external sources.

Healthy Forms of Narcissism

Another important 20th century psychologist Otto Kernberg wrote about both healthy and unhealthy levels of narcissism. He described healthy infantile and adult narcissism and then contrasted those with pathological forms of narcissism. He defined normal infantile narcissism as partly focused on external gratification since they have yet to integrate their object relations fully with their self-concept. That causes a need for admiration and validation from external sources. In other words, they want other people to admire their possessions or them, but at such an early stage of development, this is completely normal.

Kernberg described normal adult narcissism as the result of healthy object relations. That means the individual with a healthy dose of narcissism had good, positive relationships with their early caretakers, and as a result, they internalized a healthy and positive concept of self as well as that of others—the objects in object relations. Because of this integrated self-concept, these individuals possess healthy coping strategies when confronted with ambivalence, as well as the existence of both good and bad in both other people and themselves. They can readily cope with that because they regulate their self-esteem internally since they have an inner voice that can confirm they are good enough. That makes them effective actors in their life and gives them a stable moral compass, even when they are acting aggressively or expressing their sexuality.

Unhealthy Forms of Narcissism

When an infant's superego remains infantile as they grow up, the adult in that situation will still have very childish values and ideals, and that is considered pathological. It develops into a narcissistic personality disorder, which is characterized by aberrations in the expression of love for others, expression of love for self, and the individual's moral compass and superego.

The result of those aberrations includes delusions of grandeur and fantasies about excessive success with regard to beauty, love, happiness, and influence over others. The problem is that the "self-love" possessed by someone with NPD is very unstable, and because the individual still has very infantile ideals and needs, it relies almost exclusively on external sources of validation—in other words, praise from other people.

If they don't get that external validation, or they fear they won't be able to achieve their grand aspirations, they often spiral down into intense emotions of worthlessness, extreme anger, and ultimately, depression. Relationships for the narcissist then take on even more importance since they function to regulate their fragile self-esteem. Thus, they envy people who have things they don't, and that causes them to try devaluing those people and destroying their achievements, so the narcissist can perhaps feel superior. It, in essence, allows them to explain why they themselves have not achieved what this other inferior person has. They will also have no qualms about taking advantage of other people for the same reason—to feel as though they are superior. Clearly, the kind of behavior they engage in to achieve those ends makes it very difficult to form stable, long-lasting, and loving relationships.

Part of the reason the narcissist behaves in the way they do is that their difficulty with object relations has left them with no internal support for their self-esteem. They develop the exaggerated sense of self as a kind of adaptation to protect themselves from negative life experiences. As you might expect from this description, narcissism doesn't always express itself in exactly the same way. It's not a unitary concept; rather, there have been a number of narcissism categories described to help explain the nuances in its character. Let's examine a few of those.

Antisocial Narcissism

One subdivision of narcissism results in positive and negative types known as prosocial and antisocial. The antisocial narcissist is someone who is very self-centered and difficult to be around. They typically expect excessive and almost constant gratification from the people in their life. This need is not linked to their performance. In other words, they need not have accomplished something to expect that they will be admired. They also frequently exploit relationships for their own benefit, and you would likely describe this person as being in it only for themselves. They cannot consider the needs of other people in their relationships.

Prosocial Narcissism

In contrast to the antisocial narcissist, the prosocial narcissist *does* strive to do good deeds, particularly if they can do them publicly, and it is from their positive accomplishments that they expect to receive admiration and credit for their work. They are trying to make other people in their life happy, and they want to be liked. While narcissists are typically characterized by a lack of empathy, these narcissists actually use empathy to figure out what you need, so they can respond to those needs and you will praise them. That will thus get the validation they so desperately need.

These kinds of narcissists are often really fun to be around because they seem to know what you like and strive to provide that for you. Although they may be more benign than the antisocial narcissists, the problem is that they are really doing it for all the wrong reasons. They want to help others and please you not out of any sense of altruism, but so that you will praise them and give their self-esteem that required external validation they desperately seek.

Malignant Narcissism

In contrast to the prosocial narcissist, a malignant narcissist won't do anything for anyone else's benefit. These are the people who want to bring other people down to prop up their own self-esteem. That's exactly what they do too. They will lash out at you, attempt to destroy you, and are generally very thin-skinned. They see everything as an attack on them, even something as minor as a casual remark. As a result of their extremely fragile sense of self, they can become very aggressive if they believe they are being threatened, and almost everything seems threatening to them.

Kernberg described these narcissists as having a combination of narcissistic personality disorder and antisocial personality disorder. Their behavior is extremely unstable, and although they can form long-lasting relationships, it's important to realize if you're dealing with this kind of narcissist that they don't believe they are limited by something as trivial as the truth. They will readily lie, and if caught, they will become angry at you for catching them. They see the social landscape as a huge contest and are going to win at any cost.

Grandiose Narcissism

The various forms of narcissism share some common characteristics: an exaggerated sense of self-importance, a sense of entitlement, and self-centeredness, all of which produce difficulties in forming long-lasting interpersonal relationships. Thus, the categories described above can fall into this category. You can be an antisocial or malignant narcissist while also being a grandiose narcissist, for example.

Grandiose narcissists are those who overestimate their abilities, lay claim to high self-esteem (although inside is a different story), and exhibit interpersonal dominance. These are the people who will work to suppress any information that is not consistent with their image while actively promoting their positive illusions. They indulge themselves in fantasies of perfection, omnipotence, and always superiority.

These narcissists tend toward exploitative and aggressive behaviors. Typically, the more grandiose the narcissist, the more disagreeable and neurotic they are, and the more extraverted they are as well! That is to say, they actively seek out other people while loudly proclaiming their superiority and perfection to where they are neurotically obsessive and extremely disagreeable to be around.

Vulnerable (or Covert) Narcissism

This is a narcissist whom you might not recognize as such. In contrast to the grandiose narcissist, this person is less obvious in their narcissistic behaviors. They still believe themselves to be superior, but they just don't advertise it like grandiose narcissists do. These are the people who feel chronically victimized by the world because they do believe they are entitled to more than what they are getting. They still have an inflated sense of self, and they must work to maintain it, but they do that in a, well, sneakier way. They might, for example, do a good job so they will be praised for doing so.

The problem with that is they are not doing something because they genuinely want to help; rather, they expect and feel entitled to the praise that comes with the accomplishments they achieve. Of course, they never believe they are recognized enough. They still feel as though the world is failing to see how brilliant and special they truly are. They appear to have empathy for other people because they often help with a situation, but the truth is they are merely projecting the appearance of empathy so others will see how sensitive and kind they are.

Because this type of narcissist hides their true feelings and doesn't act aggressively to get their need for external validation met, they are prone to developing depression. They may feel inside that they are not being validated enough, but they don't express those feelings outwardly. Instead, they stuff them inside, which can easily lead to depressive thoughts.

A Rose by Any Other Name...

Psychologist, author, lecturer, and consultant on narcissistic disorders Elinor Greenberg answers the question on the number of narcissists out there using slightly different terms. Many of these have the same meaning as those described above but are labeled differently.

According to Greenberg, her training identified three main types of narcissists:

1. **Exhibitionist Narcissists**: These would have the same characteristics as grandiose narcissists. This is what most people picture when they think about a narcissist. These people like the spotlight and desire admiration and adoration. Greenberg labeled their self-esteem management as the GOD defense,

which is an acronym that stands for Grandiosity, Omnipotence, and Devaluation. In short, they believe themselves to be always perfect and right, and what other people think or feel simply doesn't matter. They see themselves as special and thus entitled to whatever it is they want.

2. **Closet Narcissists**: These would be the vulnerable narcissists described above. They are not comfortable being in the spotlight because they feel too vulnerable there. They still think like the exhibitionist or grandiose narcissist—they still feel entitled and special—but they get their external validation through association with special people or groups. That then makes them special. They can appear modest, but on the inside, they are lamenting how they are not being admired or recognized as much as they think they should be.

3. **Toxic Narcissists**: These are the narcissists who, like the malignant narcissist described above, want to be feared. In fact, Greenberg equates the toxic narcissist label to that of a malignant narcissist. She describes them as having a sadistic streak and enjoying devaluing and humiliating other people to cause them pain and dominate them.

Greenberg then discusses prosocial and antisocial narcissists as related to how a narcissist gets their narcissistic supply. The exhibitionistic and closet narcissists would be prosocial narcissists since they get their narcissistic supply from positive activities and achievements. They want to be the hero and have people adore them for their amazing, good deeds. They're only doing all that to get that external validation, however.

In contrast, antisocial narcissists rarely care for other people, and they don't really do anything that merits recognition. They want prestige and titles, but they don't want to do anything to get them. They are very openly egotistical since they frequently must devalue other people to demonstrate their superiority. They are completely self-serving and have no shame about that fact. Greenberg identifies another group of toxic antisocial narcissists whom she describes as "simply destructive."

Yet Another Model

Russ et al. (2008) and Caligor et al. (2015) describe yet another model for subtypes of narcissistic personality disorder. They also define three major subtypes but use some different terms.

1. **Grandiose or Overt Narcissism**: This subtype is considered to have the most problems interacting with other people. It is also the subtype that most frequently has other diagnosed psychiatric conditions, such as other types of personality disorders and substance abuse. Narcissists in this category display more anger and aggression than the other two types. These people are also less likely to ask for help, and if they do, they are more likely to disengage from treatment. The malignant narcissist as described above is part of this subtype.

2. **Fragile/Vulnerable or Covert Narcissism**: This subtype most often exists with depression and anxiety for many of the same reasons as described above. They are more vulnerable to criticism and fluctuate more between high and low self-esteem. Because they don't behave as overtly as the grandiose type, they are often missed upon diagnosis. Many clinicians diagnose depression or anxiety but fail to see the underlying narcissism that is at the root of it all. These people are preoccupied with their own perceived failures and highly sensitive nature. They still, as described previously, expect and need that external validation, but

they don't ask for it as obviously or aggressively as other types.

3. **High-Functioning or Exhibitionistic Narcissism**: This type doesn't have as many comorbidities (co-diagnoses with other conditions) as other types, and they can appear outwardly successful. They can maintain a stable sense of self-esteem, but they still have issues of entitlement and self-absorption that causes them to have problems in relationships, as they frequently exhibit exploitative and unempathetic behavior. These narcissists can destabilize when confronted with a life crisis, such as the loss of a job or a divorce, and that's when their narcissism is likely to become more evident.

Conclusion

As you can see from the various terms and types identified by different experts over time, there is some controversy over just what constitutes pathological narcissism. Some experts, for example, argue that high-functioning narcissists shouldn't fall under the rubric of NPD; rather, they should simply be described as people with narcissistic traits. Others argue that the latter category would encompass almost everyone. The issue has not been resolved to the satisfaction of most experts, and therefore, the description of NPD in the DSM-5 simply describes it as a homogeneous personality disorder with evidence toward overt and covert subtypes.

What is clear is that narcissism exists on a spectrum, and all of the subtypes share certain features, specifically a lack of empathy and strong need for external validation. These behaviors are driven by unstable, fragile self-esteem, even if the narcissist insists otherwise. It is clearly a complex mental condition and one that deserves more investigation. One of the areas of research is in the role of culture, which we'll examine in more depth in the next chapter.

Chapter Four: The Modern Era of Narcissism, Entitlement, and Toxic People

"Since narcissists deep down feel themselves to be faultless, it is inevitable that when they are in conflict with the world, they will invariably perceive the conflict as the world's fault." —M. Scott Peck

Many experts point to several factors in our culture itself that encourage narcissistic behavior. They even call it an epidemic of narcissism and argue that it is seen at the highest levels of government, but is that true? Are we becoming—or have we always been—a narcissistic culture? Why does it seem like we're seeing so many more examples of narcissism, people who feel entitled, and other kinds of toxic people?

Public Comments about Cultural Narcissism

With 20 years' experience in corporate America, Roger describes five of the most important lessons he has learned. Most of them support or encourage narcissistic traits. His five biggest lessons are:

1. *The ends always justify the means;*

2. *There is no meritocracy;*

3. *You will have to learn corporate speak;*

4. *Other people are driven by their drivers;*

5. *It's almost impossible to turn down a promotion. Therefore, people get promoted until they reach a job they cannot do.*

How do they encourage narcissism? Well, they encourage—through reward—many of the behaviors typical of NPD. These include a self-serving attitude (numbers 1, 3, 4, and 5), the idea that image is everything regardless of reality (1, 2, 3, and 5), and the normalization of an unstable self-esteem that every narcissist hides inside (1, 2, 4, and 5). These are, indeed, the hallmarks of the corporate world, and not just in the United States.

Victor, a business owner who has had three narcissistic partners in her life, writes, *"Society is becoming more narcissistic. I have noticed this especially over the last seven years. Look at social media and how people have an "in your face", and a "I don't care" attitude. People these days sue others over just about anything. Look at the trash on TV, like reality shows... Our society encourages negative, self-absorbed, and aggressive behaviors."*

Anne writes, *"The answer is simple: social media. Today, most social communication is done through social media (mainly Facebook and Instagram). You can be any kind of person you want and show only what you wish people to see. Feeling depressed? Looking for attention? All you have to do is post an attractive selfie to fish for compliments or post some aspect of your life and make it look "perfect." Watch the likes and comments flood in, praising you and making you feel better about yourself. It's a cycle. People can manipulate the wording of their posts to leave some kind of subtle message self-glorifying themselves."*

It appears that people do see an increase in narcissistic behaviors, generally on a cultural level, but what does the empirical evidence say for such a trend? And, if it is true that our culture is becoming more narcissistic, why is that so?

In an individualistic culture, the narcissist is God's gift to the world. In a collectivist society, the narcissist is God's gift to the collective.

-Christopher Lasch

The Science of Narcissistic Cultures

It certainly seems like there is a strong cultural link to narcissistic behaviors. Sociologists and anthropologists make a distinction between individualistic cultures versus collectivistic cultures. The former emphasizes the importance and independence of the individual, whereas the latter emphasizes the community over the individual. In general, narcissism scores are higher in cultures identified as individualistic (the US is one big example) compared to those that are more collectivistic (China is a good example here).

To test that hypothesis, Vater et al. (2018) conducted a study that utilized the Narcissistic Personality Inventory (NPI) and Pathological Narcissism Inventory (PNI) in order to assess the incidence of grandiose and vulnerable narcissism, as well as low versus high self-esteem ratings (using the Rosenberg Self-Esteem Scale, or RSE) in 1,025 German individuals. The data was analyzed with respect to both age and place of birth. The idea was to study the results of those individuals who grew up in the former East Germany (a collectivistic culture) compared to those who grew up in West Germany (an individualistic culture).

The researchers (Vater et al., 2018) found that the data indicated higher frequencies of grandiose narcissism combined with lower levels of self-esteem in individuals who grew up in West Germany compared to East Germany. They also found no significant difference in the levels of either grandiose or vulnerable narcissism, nor self-esteem in those who had entered school after the reunification of Germany in 1989. Their results may suggest some empirical evidence for the role of culture in the rates of narcissism and levels of self-esteem.

That begs the question of the role of modern capitalistic cultures in nurturing narcissism. As mentioned previously, Campbell and Twenge (2013) argued that there is an epidemic of narcissism in modern Western cultures. They found evidence for that in the increased use of personal pronouns related to the individual—like I and me—versus the use of those pronouns that would signify a group of people, like we and us. They also noted that it was often reflected in song lyrics that focused more on the self versus the group. They are not alone in their findings.

Newsom et al. (2003) found that there has been an increase in the frequency of endorsements by adolescents for the statement, "I am an important person" from 12 percent in 1963 to 77-80 percent in 1992. Twenge et al. (2012) also found a significant increase in the use of certain narcissistic phrases like, "I am the greatest," between 1960 and 2008. Uhls and Greenfield (2011) found a stronger desire for fame in TV shows. All of this strongly suggests that there might be an increase in narcissism in individualistic cultures.

Along with all these investigations—which all demonstrate a potential role of culture in nurturing narcissistic characteristics—there is evidence that NPI scores for grandiose narcissism may be increasing over time in the United States. Twenge and Campbell (2008) found that between 1979 and 2006, the NPI scores were 30 percent higher for grandiose narcissism. Although there has been criticism of the NPI as an indicator for narcissism, its flaws may have resulted in an *underestimation* of the problem, and relatively recent research into the efficacy of the NPI in identifying narcissistic traits associated with NPD has found it to be a strong match to expert ratings of the problem (Miller et al., 2011; Miller et al., 2014).

Still, the NPI is better at detecting grandiose narcissism, and thus, the Pathological Narcissism Inventory (PNI) was developed to help identify both grandiose and vulnerable narcissism (Pincus et al., 2009). It appears to be a useful tool for assessing various types of pathological narcissism, and it has been used successfully to identify increases in both grandiose and vulnerable narcissism in various studies (Vater et al., 2018).

Because self-esteem—identified as the global evaluation of self—is an important part of diagnosing narcissism, it is thus also another major aspect of evaluating the rise of NPD. The relationship of self-esteem to NPD is nuanced, given that the narcissistic individual might lay claim to having high self-esteem, but in reality, that is a facade. The narcissist is frequently projecting a false sense of confidence that is protecting what is ultimately a frail self-esteem. Still, given that the narcissist claims to have a healthy self-esteem, self-reported scores of high self-esteem might be expected to rise with the incidence of narcissism. And it is true that self-esteem is increasing throughout the Western world. Gentile et al. (2010) found that self-esteem scores in middle school students in the United States were significantly higher in the mid-2000s compared to the late 1980s. Twenge (2015) found the same was true for college students between 1968 and 1994.

Cultural Features that Encourage Narcissism

The research strongly supports the idea that a culture can be narcissistic, but that begs the question—what are the features of culture that act to encourage narcissism? Let's examine this topic by discussing two views of the connection between culture and narcissism.

Cultures of Narcissism

The first theoretical approach claims that the link between culture and narcissism is due to how cultures are organized to promote narcissism in the individual. The proponents of this approach would argue that the increases seen in individual cases of NPD are due to structural changes in culture. The argument goes that society is a strong force in shaping the individual's psyche. This is seen most vividly in the tension created through societal pressures, which are often contradictory to individual actions that would promote self-preservation. For example, although an individual might want to steal money to help them survive, societal pressures may work to keep them from doing so.

The tension created from these contradictory pressures results in the withdrawal of certain parts of the ego into the individual's unconscious mind. By pushing those culturally objectionable parts of the ego into the subconscious realm, the individual can then fool themselves into believing the illusion of harmony between what they truly desire and the reality of what they can actually do; in other words, they accept that there is harmony between the pleasure they seek and the reality of their life. This sets up a causal connection between culture and any personality disorders that develop as a result of that tension (Grubner, 2017).

Narcissistic Cultures

The second approach assumes that there is an analogy between culture and the individual, such that cultures can be described in psychological terms. This approach would posit, therefore, that it is possible for the culture itself to be narcissistic. The evidence for this, the proponents would argue, is found in institutions, cultural products, works of art, the media, etc. Analyzing the products of culture and its institutions, then, would allow one to describe new developments and gain new insights into the culture itself.

Freud wrote about this kind of cultural theory, and he argued that cultures, like the developing human, go through stages of development. In this view, primitive cultures would share certain characteristics, like narcissistic tendencies, with young children and neurotics. Freud believed neuroses were the result of fixations during the early stages of psychosexual development, and thus, neurotics retained several childish characteristics.

Drawing on the work of anthropologists in the early 20th century, Freud interpreted their descriptions of primitive cultures in this light. For example, animism is a common feature of so-called "primitive" cultures, and Freud equated the use of magic as a means of controlling the world with omnipotence of thoughts that resulted from mistaking an ideal connection for one that is real. In that case, the "real" connection would be acknowledging one's powerlessness in certain situations.

Freud goes on to describe the more advanced stages of cultures, which are increasingly being characterized by objective thought and science. But relevant to our discussion here is that the animistic phase of culture would be analogous to narcissistic phases of human development. In this view, those "primitive" cultures are more narcissistic in their concept of the world because they express a belief in causal connections between their thoughts and desires and the reality of the outside world.

A Combination of Theories

Since the proposal of these theoretical approaches, new theories have emerged that reflect aspects of both models. These new approaches seek to address criticism of each model. For example, with respect to the first, though it is possible to see connections between cultural values and certain pathological conditions, it is difficult to establish a direct connection. Some researchers have even argued that the perceived increase in narcissism isn't real. Rather, the increase is the result of a shift in attention on certain personality types that were previously considered normal. These are now classified as abnormal, and thus, it appears there has been an increase. In reality, these personality types always existed at the same levels; they just weren't considered abnormal. It's similar to the argument about increased access to national and even international media. Is there really an increase in certain crimes, or is there just an increase in that which has been reported?

The second model has faced criticism because it is overly subject to changes in ideology because it promotes the use of diseases to describe society. By doing this, it is possible to exploit certain diseases—or in this case, a mental condition—for ideological purposes. Examples include the claim that people who got AIDS were being punished by God. When a disease or condition then becomes laden with symbolism, as we might see happening with recent political developments and narcissism, then it ignores the real causal elements behind the disease itself. This has occurred with TB and cancer as well, and it can slow progress toward understanding the causes. In light of this criticism, to relegate the increase in narcissism at the individual level to reflecting a selfish culture is to ignore the genuine causes of the problem at the individual level. This can also slow the advancement of treatments for the condition.

New theoretical models that offer more nuanced examination of the interplay between culture and narcissism are attempting to integrate these ideas. Though they still have their limitations, they can offer some insight into how cultural elements work to encourage individual narcissism that may have begun with childhood experiences.

Corporate Capitalism and Narcissism

Lasch (1979) deals at length with the relevances of narcissism as a syndrome of modern society. He examines recent developments in the culture of the United States and how those resulted in changes in the American social structure, which would ultimately be responsible for the increase in incidences of NPD. He concludes that when capitalism overcame feudalism, governments became more impersonal and bureaucratic in order to suit the needs of corporate capitalism.

During this process of cultural change, individuals are no longer the recipients of generational knowledge regarding how to meet their basic needs: raise children, produce foods, and deal with matters of health and age. Instead, that knowledge becomes increasingly the property of corporations—corporations that grow food, socialize and educate children, and treat illness. Because of this, criminals are increasingly seen as victims of society or individual family environments, and therefore, there is no real individual responsibility for their actions. At the same time, the advertising industry projects desires that can ultimately never be satisfied; instead, projecting an image of fulfillment becomes the goal.

Based on this assumption of cultural change and the downstream effects of that change, Lasch (1979) proposes two models for how personality is shaped. The first is that the individual concept of self is regressed by the decline in parental authority to a narcissistic, infantile, grandiose, and empty version. If, on the other hand, there is a realistic parental authority involved in the life of the individual—one that has not been usurped by the corporate model—then the individual would develop a more reality-oriented, stable sense of self. In this way, the levels of narcissism become an indicator of individual experiences with their culture, and the level at which it has been a part of their development over older, more traditional authority figures (i.e., parental versus corporate authority figures).

Although this model integrates the role of the individual's family environment in either exercising or delegating authority to cultural norms, Lasch (1979) proposes another model that he argues is more reflective of the actual reason for rises in levels of narcissism. The second model assumes that cultures play a role in fostering certain personality traits by either rewarding them if they are in line with specific cultural values or creating a dilemma where the individual has to resolve traits that contradict those cultural values. In other words, the individual has to have the strength of character to buck cultural values and norms and find justification for doing so, or they simply have to reorient their behavior to be more in line with those cultural values. This sets up a situation where the culture is narcissistic, and an individual who is not can be made to feel abnormal and perhaps even ill.

So, how might cultures promote narcissistic personality traits? Let's look at three main ways that Lasch (1979) argues this can happen.

1. **Financial and symbolic rewards**: People who exhibit certain narcissistic personality traits get better paying jobs, are rewarded with promotions into management positions, and are admired by their peers for those reasons.

2. **Narcissism as a coping mechanism**: Because cultures can use scientifically determined norms as a method of determining good versus bad behavior, people are constantly scrutinizing themselves against those norms. Are you a proper weight? Are you aging well? Are you healthy? This can cause anxiety and fear around not conforming to those standards, and indeed, those who do not conform are ridiculed. It prevents people from using critical thinking skills to distance themselves from normative thinking. In other words, they lose the ability to apply common sense, analyze their situation, and act on what they discover. It's easier, therefore, to project a narcissistic image of perfection than try to go your own way.

3. **Virtual realities**: The ubiquitous nature of virtual realities—be it social media, the internet in general, or even mass media and advertising (which is primarily what Lasch was talking about in 1979)—means that our sense of reality and place in it can easily be blurred. Recent events have demonstrated how easy it is for mass media to replace the traditional requirements for what is considered false or true information. It no longer matters whether the information in question is credible. In the

virtual world, the logic of make-believe rules the day.

Conclusion

So, what does all of this mean? Well, the evidence strongly suggests that narcissism is on the increase; it's not just an artifact with increasing attention on the subject. This increase certainly has a connection to changes we've seen culturally. It does appear that our culture rewards certain narcissistic traits, and within that context, if you don't conform to what your society expects of you, you must either find the internal fortitude to go against that powerful force or use narcissism to project an image that's in line with societal expectations. Lastly, narcissism is also in line with certain trends that we've seen dramatic increases in within the last 40 years, and that is the "spectacularization" of society. Everything has become a spectacle. Reality shows are all the rage, and the more dramatic, the better. This love of the spectacle has also seeped into our political reality.

Still, it can't all be explained by a narcissistic culture. There are still individual factors to consider, and it's kind of like the famous question: which came first, the chicken or the egg? Is the culture actually creating narcissistic individuals, or are narcissistic people giving the culture the form it has? And, what about those who do have a stable enough ego to resist the lure of cultural norms that go against their own internalized values? Most likely, the answer lies somewhere in between. It is likely more the result of a culture that glorifies certain narcissistic tendencies and its interaction with individuals who have developed those tendencies to a greater degree, perhaps even to the level of pathology. But how does narcissism develop in the individual? We'll examine that in the next chapter.

Chapter Five: How Narcissism Develops to Create a Toxic Person

"Love doesn't die a natural death. Love has to be killed, either by neglect or narcissism." —Frank Salvato

It's hard to understand how someone can become so toxic if you've never experienced that before. Perhaps it's best to remember that, as Michael writes, *"On the most fundamental level, a narcissist is, above all else, a human being."* In his compassionate treatment of the subject, he also notes that the story of that narcissist is something that is much more profound than any label can convey. Still, how is NPD diagnosed, and what causes it? How does it develop?

How is NPD Diagnosed?

Psychologist Elinor Greenberg first describes the symptoms that would lead her to diagnose someone with NPD. It is something she refers to as the narcissistic pattern, which essentially means that the individual's childhood left them believing that either you're a winner, or you're a loser. To be a winner, you need to be seen by other people as being special, unique, perfect, and even omnipotent. You always have to be right, and you must win every contest, or you're a loser. The goal in their mind is to rise to the top of any hierarchy that exists in any area of their life. If they can achieve this, then they will be entitled to special treatment.

If, on the other hand, you are not able to win every contest that comes your way, then you're a loser. You won't be seen as special; instead, you'll be considered worthless garbage, and your only reason for existence will be to serve the winners. Healthy people don't define winning and losing in these terms, and they see gradations of everything in between the "winner" and the "loser." Greenberg states that to diagnose someone, she specifically looks for the following 7 signs:

1. **A Split Self**: This is the idea that narcissists see themselves as either a winner or a loser, nothing in between. They divide their world into a binary reality for themselves and other

people. You're either special, unique, and entitled, or you're irredeemably flawed and worthless. There is nothing in between.

2. **The "GOD" Defense**: This is what Greenberg looks for in their behavior- grandiosity, a sense of omnipotence, and that is combined with devaluation of others. GOD: Grandiosity, Omnipotence, and Devaluation, applies to all narcissists except covert narcissists. In that type, you don't see these traits openly, though they are going on inside.

3. **Lack of Whole Object Relations (WOR) and Lack of Object Constancy**: WOR is where you can see yourself and other people as having both bad and good traits. You have parts of your personality and behavior that are liked and parts that are not liked. Such makes up the whole you. Narcissists lack that. They cannot allow for anything that is bad or disliked, or else they become a loser. Object constancy refers to the ability to still have positive feelings for someone, even when you feel hurt, disappointed, or angry with them. Again, narcissists lack this ability. If you've hurt them, you're dead to them. That's in part because they can't see that a person can have both good and bad traits.

4. **Status Hierarchies**: For a narcissist, everything is arranged vertically, and thus, they rank each person they meet in terms of their own favorite status hierarchy. These hierarchies might be based on power, beauty, intelligence, fashion, money, wit, fame, or athleticism.

5. **Expression of Contempt**: This refers to how frequently the individual expresses contempt for other people. Narcissists do this frequently and more openly than most others do.

6. **Shame-Based, Self-Hating Depressions**: Because the narcissist is protecting their low self-esteem, they feel very threatened by criticism. They frequently feel shame, and when that happens, they will spiral into a self-loathing depression. Since they don't possess whole object relations (WOR), they can't look at any criticism and either learn from it for the future or reflect that they have done good things in the past. They simply feel totally worthless and see it as being a permanent situation.

7. **Extra Sensitive**: Narcissists are very sensitive people. They feel hurt by even the most minor slights or criticism. Most people wouldn't even notice such small slights, but the narcissist

feels deeply embarrassed and is likely to lash out in anger.

If you're dealing with a narcissist in your life, you likely recognize these symptoms of NPD, but how did it develop? Why are they that way?

How Does NPD Develop?

According to Greenberg, it's a byproduct of their early childhood environment. Of course, all children want their parents' attention and approval. That's only natural, but children will also adapt to their home environments, and unfortunately, for some, the only way to adapt is to become a narcissist. Greenberg notes that there are three situations she most frequently hears about from her narcissistic clients. These include the following:

1. One or Both Parents are Narcissists

If your parents are narcissists, they will model narcissistic behaviors and values for their children. It's that simple. For a child with one or two narcissistic parents, that means that achievement, status, and image are the most valuable things in their home. They will only get positive attention from their parents if they are doing better than their peers, ranking high, and achieving their goals. They will only be praised when they are winners.

For the narcissistic parent, love is, in fact, conditional. Their children are only showered with love when they succeed. They aren't concerned with knowing "who" their children really are or even what they like and need. They are concerned with how their family appears to other people—that is, the image the family projects. When their child makes the family look good by succeeding, they reward them with praise and love. If they don't make the family look good, however, they are punished, shamed, guilted, and made to feel unloved in every way.

2. Devaluation by Narcissistic Parents

Devaluation is a hallmark behavior for narcissism, and it doesn't matter if you're a child. If you make mistakes, your narcissistic parent will humiliate you publicly and castigate you privately. You will be held up as a disappointment to your family, and it will be expected that you will be a failure because they believe you to be a loser.

When a child is experiencing this devaluation, they can react in one of two ways. They might give up and accept defeat. These types typically become substance abusers as they try to escape their feelings of shame. Other children will choose to fight back and prove that their parents are wrong about them. They will pursue success at all costs. They will frequently step on anyone in their way. Their childhood makes them hard and uncaring.

3. The Exhibitionist's Admirer

This is often how covert narcissists are created. In this situation, the parents reward the child for admiring them and serving their needs. These children are taught narcissistic values, but they are not allowed to exhibit them. They have a very specific role in the family: they are to worship (uncritically) their narcissistic parent(s). They are not supposed to equal their parent's achievement, and by no means should they ever surpass them.

In my bestselling book, _My Toxic Husband: Loving and Breaking Up with a Narcissistic Man—Start Your Psychopath-free Life Now_, I recount my story of meeting and marrying a narcissist. Of course, I didn't know he was a narcissist at the time. In fact, he seemed like the perfect man for me. But he soon revealed his true self, and as I began to understand what was happening, I realized that his mother was also a narcissist, and that's how I found out firsthand how narcissistic parents can create narcissistic children. One of the things I found myself wondering often was how he was actually feeling on the inside; what was he thinking and feeling?

BASED ON A TRUE STORY

MY TOXIC HUSBAND

LOVING AND BREAKING UP WITH A NARCISSISTIC MAN - START YOUR PSYCHOPATH-FREE LIFE NOW!

ELENA MIRO

What's Happening Internally?

According to Greenberg, narcissism is an adaptation to a childhood environment where you were taught or modeled narcissistic behaviors. This really makes sense from the perspective that what a child sees in their home is completely normal to them. They may not like it, but they don't have any other experience to compare it with, and thus, they see it as normal. They also adapt to what's going on. They have to in order to survive.

Other researchers also point to object relations as an area that is pathological in narcissists. When you can't see that there is both good and bad in people, including yourself, you develop a negative or ambivalent internalized mental image of yourself and other people. It's a given that you'll fail at some point in your childhood, if for no other reason than you haven't done the task at hand before. When that happens to the child of a toxic parent, you'll be berated and devalued, putting you squarely in the loser category.

As the child sees the world in toxic, binary terms, it's also inevitable that they will be let down at some point by their early relationships. This prompts an adaptive mechanism to develop in the child. They try to create a situation where they don't need other people. They want to be self-sufficient, but to achieve that, they must create what is inevitably a pathological union of self—the ideal self—and the ideal object. In this fantasy unification, the narcissist has everything they need without other people.

The problem is that they have effectively taken their superego—the ideal self—and unified it with their real self. When that happens, the superego is actually weakened, causing it to become overly strict. These are the people with a severely negative inner critic. The result is that the narcissist can't possibly pass the superego's high standards, and failure is both inevitable, and debilitating. If they can pass the high standards of their strict superego, they will believe that no one is better than they are, but it's not worth the crash that happens when they fail. Because they don't have healthy object relations to fall back on, they can't comfort themselves with thoughts like, "I'll get 'em next time," and they can't accept the comfort that might otherwise come from others. Instead, they are at the mercy of their wildly unstable and incredibly strict superego.

A Few Insights from the Trenches

It can help to illustrate these concepts to hear from people who are narcissists or dealing with them in their lives.

Pamela writes the following about her narcissistic husband:

"I would say that a narcissist's inside feelings are probably a form of simple disappointment or elation when they are successful or unsuccessful in reaching a goal or performing a task. Their feelings about a relationship are mainly observations without being connected on a deep level."

Ana, who is a narcissist, writes this:

"How I feel about myself is… there's this cardboard cutout of this idealized omnipotent, Hollywood, made-up person I want to be. And sometimes, in my imagination, I can approximate.

This person is, of course, ageless and transcendentally beautiful, desired by many, brilliant, polymathic, courageous, daring—a maverick. Just smash together the plots to some female James Bond, Lara Croft Tomb Raider, and whatever other nonsense for some unreal female anime out there, and that's the person I not only want to be but feel I have to be.

But of course, daily reality impinges upon that vision, even in the simple fact of confronting a mirror and realizing I'm 'not all that.' Or that all the years I could have dedicated to a useful craft were so misspent that I am not particularly great at anything. Or when people at my job give me the side-eye because the shit I overpromised I way failed to deliver.

And then I feel like the scummiest garbage that ever had to suck oxygen, and I wonder how much more of this embodied existence I am supposed to have to tolerate. How many more years of being this.... thing?

So that's a pretty Crazy 8 of absolute immutable, omnipotent Might, followed by the murkiest depths of supreme self-rejection.

At this stage of my life, I have achieved some critical distance from this, my existential state, and mostly just roll my eyes at whatever caca my mind punishes me with. I have come to terms with the fact that I am, and always have been, a being of the most exquisite mediocrity, and that's just the way it is— that's just the way it has to be. So I focus on trying to enjoy life's simple pleasures and show up for what there is to show up for, with the best goodwill and commitment of which I am capable.

But it definitely requires a constant, conscious decision because at any moment, I am liable to slip into my old tricks."

Conclusion

With Ana's words, it's possible to see the pain that the narcissist suffers with on a daily basis. They behave in a toxic way, no doubt, but it's because they constantly feel the toxicity inside. That's because they were exposed to this way of being when their personality was just beginning to form. It's here that people who suffer at the hands of a narcissist might be able to find the compassion it takes to remain as a positive force in their life. That's a difficult road to choose, but it's one that adds immeasurable value to the life of the person suffering from NPD.

In this chapter, we've seen how narcissism develops and is diagnosed, but how can someone who's not an expert spot a narcissist? That's what we'll examine in the next chapter: just how their inner toxicity is presented to the world.

Chapter Six: How Do You Know They're a Narcissist?

"Have you ever been in a relationship with an individual who demands your attention incessantly and becomes depressed, sulky, and even full of rage if your attention goes elsewhere? This is one of the earliest warning signs of a narcissist." —Melanie Tonia Evans

As we've seen, everyone possesses some narcissistic traits, and that is a healthy thing, but how can you know that you're dealing with a pathological narcissist? I certainly didn't have a clue that my ex-husband was a narcissist when I first met him. It took a while to see his darker side, and when that happened, I was so confused about why he was acting that way that I really didn't know what to think. I eventually discovered that it was narcissism, but how do you know that the problem you might be dealing with is really a situation of narcissism as opposed to some other kind of mental condition? How can you know you're dealing with a narcissist?

Stories from the Veterans of Narcissism

Richard writes the following about realizing his girlfriend was a narcissist:

"I unwittingly became exactly what the narcissist was looking for. I had just gotten out of a relationship of 13 years with a very controlling, jealous person. It had really changed me, but I was starting to get better. That's when I met my narcissist. She was actually a friend of mine, or I thought she was a friend. When she found out I had broken up with my old girlfriend, she wasted no time. She started love bombing me, and I was vulnerable at the time. I fell for her quickly. At that time, I didn't know what NPD was, but I soon found out.

I had never seen anyone change as quickly and in the way that she did. It was bizarre. She became so unpredictable, flying into a rage at a moment's notice. I began to try to find answers, and I soon learned I was dealing with a narcissist. By that time, I was hooked on her. I kept thinking I could help her, change her. I have since found out nothing could be further from the truth. I was just a puppet in her show, and unless I got out, that would always be the case. She had looked for someone just like me—someone down, lonely, and who needed someone to feel whole again. I'm trying to move forward again, and I won't stop trying, but I know the experience has changed me forever."

Jackie writes the following about her ex:

"I didn't know he was a narcissist until after breaking up with each other. I was trauma bonded and at my worst. Depressed, lonely, penniless, confused, heartbroken, angry at all he put me through. He was all I could think about. I was truly mindfucked and feeling crazy. Someone I knew that I met through my ex suggested I look up "sociopath" online. I did and I found Profile of the Sociopath *by R. Preston McAfee. My ex's behavior suddenly made sense to me. It made me realize he never loved me like he had told me; I'd been conned. He wasn't as stupid as I had thought; he played me from the start. I was the one who I suddenly thought was the stupid one.*

All those times he screwed up, pissed me off, stole something, lied to me, denied, finger-pointed blame, smirked, cried, hit me, said horrible things to me, committed forgery, identity theft that I thought about made it all clear, finally, to me... There is no one in his life he hasn't lied to or stolen from. He lies, charms, and manipulates his way through life. He never stops. When I'd figure out one horrible thing he did to me, he already had done three more things. It was all-consuming for me. Anxiety and panic, PTSD and paranoia, high emotions and drama all the time."

Joan writes this about her narcissistic mother:

"I have to tell you that I really didn't know what narcissism was. In fact, when I decided to stop all contact with my family, I didn't know I was addressing something that has been written about and discussed on the web. I didn't know that other people had the same thing happen to them when I had the notion to just put a stop to the negative feelings I was experiencing. It was around New Year's several years back that I had an epiphany about being taken advantage of. I don't know what happened to me; I just got really aware of how I was feeling. I'd just turned 50, and maybe that was the wake up call. I am not sure exactly, but when I heard her voice on the answering machine, I just had this awful feeling and I didn't want to talk to her. I never really did; it was like a torture. I could never share good news with her because she would try to deflate my happiness by downplaying it or acting jealous. And when those phone calls would come in, she would sound as if she were about to die. I didn't know that she was mentally ill necessarily because I'd become so accustomed to their conditioning that I didn't allow myself to feel how wrong it was. They took advantage of me and psychologically abused me, but I didn't realize the full extent of the abuse until I just got really angry about it.

Then it was like, enough already—just enough. I blocked her calls. I went through a long period of depression over it. I remember walking my dog all by myself and feeling like crying. Then, after about six months, I gave in and called her. She acted as if she didn't even think it was a big deal. That was the first red flag. And she put on this pretense of crying, but by then, I could tell it was fake. When she'd pull temper tantrums long ago, I recall there were no tears. And then she picked up where she left off, making snide remarks designed to make me feel guilty for not going down to visit them when I said a million times that I can't drive anymore due to my macular degenerative disease and the fact that the car is 19 years old and unreliable.

Didn't matter. She really didn't want to see me. She just wanted to have someone to manipulate, and I found out that means I was scapegoated all along and didn't know it. So I never got mad or anything, I just pretended that it didn't bother me, and when I hung up, I thought about what happened and blocked the number. No one tells you what is going to happen when you do this. Keep in mind, this is a couple of years before I found Quora and other feeds devoted to the subject of narcissistic abuse.

She tried everything in the book… sending 'flying monkeys' in a state of panic… i.e. letters, phone calls from cell phones that they purchased with different numbers. Paranoid, I began to think they would come to my house. I called the police, and they were nice enough to say that they would call them on our behalf to have them warned about a possible restraining order. That was a few years back… now, just four days ago, cops came to my house and said that a relative told them to come here because they suspected that my husband was preventing me from getting in contact with them. So there is no telling what they will do."

Trends Indicating Narcissism

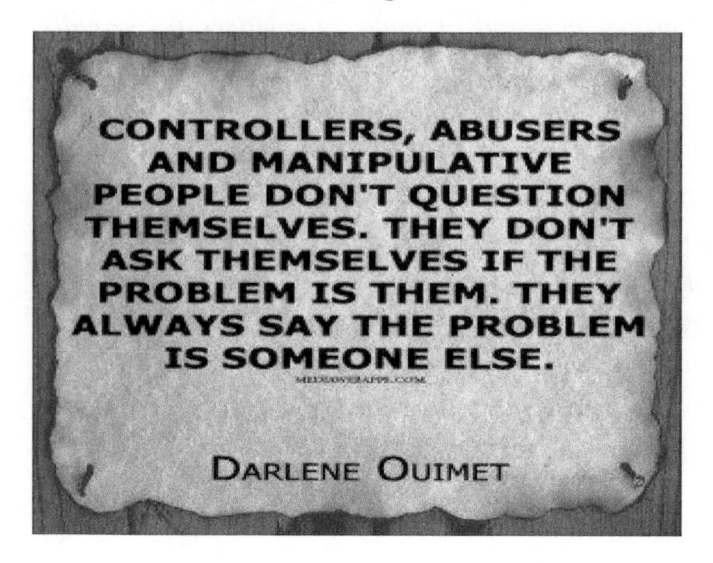

> **CONTROLLERS, ABUSERS AND MANIPULATIVE PEOPLE DON'T QUESTION THEMSELVES. THEY DON'T ASK THEMSELVES IF THE PROBLEM IS THEM. THEY ALWAYS SAY THE PROBLEM IS SOMEONE ELSE.**
>
> MEDIEOVERAPPS.COM
>
> DARLENE OUIMET

As you read the stories above, you can start to see common themes within. They were all vulnerable when they were taken advantage of, had trouble understanding the behaviors of the narcissist in their life, and were manipulated to varying degrees by behaviors they didn't fully understand.

It took them time to understand that what they were dealing with was narcissism. Most people have encountered at least one narcissist in their life. It might be the friend who always directs the conversation back to herself, the coworker who brags about their accomplishments even when you know they're taking credit for someone else's work, or the lover who starts out great but suddenly changes into someone you don't recognize.

Of course, narcissists, like people of all stripes, are on a continuum. Some are worse than others, and some show their narcissistic tendencies, whereas others are experts at hiding them. One thing is true of all of them: they're draining to deal with. They make you feel tired and unsatisfied with the interaction. You might even feel confused by what just happened. But is there a way to identify for sure that you're dealing with a narcissist? Well, the following characteristics are common among narcissists.

They Seem Likable at First

Narcissists are actually very good at first impressions. They often seem very personable and charismatic. My husband definitely seemed like the best man I had ever met. He was charming, supportive, generous, and just wonderful, but it was all a facade. Because they can be so charming, they tend to do well in job interviews. They will shower you with praise, extol their best characteristics, and seem generally well-adjusted. They appear to have a healthy self-esteem and can often do very impressive things. You'll like them, and you'll be impressed when you first meet them.

The problem is that their charisma and charm just doesn't last, and when it turns negative, it happens fast. That's why so many people, like Richard above, will describe them as changing so quickly. It is just that quick too. One minute, they're supportive and loving, and the next, they're unleashing a load of narcissistic rage on you. It's quite surprising and even frightening. You don't want it to be true, and so, you make excuses. You might think they're just having a bad day or that they're under stress, but the over-the-top reaction is more than that.

Their initial charm is often why they are frequently in leadership roles and positions of power. They get in, give a great first impression, and then before you know it, they're leading the team. That's typically when you find out your boss is a narcissist. You might wonder how they can manage that, but the truth is, the narcissist wants to be in a position of power. They want to be seen as leaders and admired for their leadership. That doesn't mean they are good leaders, but they are much more likely to end up in leadership roles because that's what they are working for.

When the Change Happens

Typically, by the time the change in their attitude happens, you're in deep. You've been thoroughly impressed by them, whether it's a romantic or professional relationship. They start off great, but then they change. Suddenly, you realize all they really want to talk about is themselves, and no matter the conversation you're having, they always steer it back to something having to do with their life.

You've just told them you have cancer, and they start talking about their new car. You're breaking up with your spouse? They'll be happy to tell you all about how they just met the man or woman of their dreams. And they will expect that you will be happy for them and admire their charm. If you don't respond in the way they believe you should, you'll soon find yourself on the business end of their narcissistic rage.

Their rage is sudden, harsh, and loud. They have no compunctions about dressing you down in public either, and they can go from someone who seemed to be so caring and kind to someone who is ice cold in an instant. It's genuinely startling to witness the change that occurs. I ran into that with my ex-husband. He would be fine one minute, and then just start berating me the next. Though you might initially resist believing there is something really wrong, or that they have some kind of personality disorder, you'll soon witness more symptoms that will convince you that they are a narcissist. Here are several things you'll likely see in their behavior.

- **Name-dropping**: They like to emphasize their importance, and to do that, they will drop the names of people who are famous or well-known in their field. They get a large boost of self-esteem from being associated with people they think are important, and they will let you know of the association so you can admire them accordingly. If you fail to do so, you will likely be ridiculed and devalued.

- **It's all about image**: Because the narcissist has no internal validation that can make their self-esteem unstable, they get their validation externally. That means they must appear to be great, intelligent, kind, loving, supportive, beautiful, and anything else they value. Their image is everything to them because it is from their image that they derive their sense of self. They will always take great care in ensuring they look clean and well-groomed. Physical attraction is a big part of their image. They will also do whatever they can to prove how intelligent they are, even if that means ridiculing other people. They will go out of their way to appear successful.

- **Don't dare to criticize**: Because it's all about image, narcissists are very strongly averse to any kind of criticism, even with that which can be considered the most gentle of advice. They are hypersensitive to it, and being criticized will either cause them to defend themselves by devaluing and belittling the person who has criticized them, or they may spiral into a deep depression. Part of the problem is their need for external validation. They get their sense of self from sources outside of themselves, and to be criticized is basically to have their self destroyed.

- **Blaming and shaming**: Because of their need for external validation and fear of criticism, they are always ready to blame and shame others for any problems they encounter or cause in their life. It's never their fault, and there is never any need for them to improve. They can always point to someone else who caused their problem, and they will never admit even a role in making any mistakes. Instead, they are full of excuses and blame.

- **It's personal**: Everything to a narcissist is personal, and this is particularly true for covert narcissists who aren't as outwardly obvious in their behavior. Remember, they lack object relations, and so, if you're criticizing them, it's personal. It's about the very core of their being. They can't see that there is good and bad in everyone, so if you're saying they did something bad, you're saying they ARE bad. And when they believe that's the case, they are ready to react with a dose of narcissistic rage to put you in your place.

- **They leave a trail of wreckage in their wake**: If the person you think might be a narcissist has a history of numerous bad relationships and/or work experiences, that's a big red flag that they are a narcissist. Remember, it's personal and they're never to blame, so if they're telling you all about their crazy ex-girlfriends—all 10 of them—or their seven crazy ex-boyfriends, that's a big sign they're a narcissist. Again, this is related to the lack of object relations. They can't see that there is good and bad in an ex. So, if you see that they only speak negatively of their ex-partners, consider that they might be a narcissist.

- **They cheat and lie regularly**: Narcissists are known to lie as part of their manipulation tactics, but they are also more likely to cheat in a relationship. They don't have the ability to put someone else's feelings above their own, and they need to be externally validated. So, when someone shows a romantic interest in them, they will pursue them to get their self-esteem fix. They need that admiration and adoration, and there's nothing quite like the beginning stages of a new relationship to make you feel adored.

- **They seem so confident**: In fact, the narcissist is confident to the point of arrogance. Now, underneath is an unstable self-esteem, but the narcissist themselves doesn't know that. They have become so adept at projecting an air of confidence that they have forgotten it's a false facade. They believe their own projection, and they thoroughly allow themselves to get lost in the story they've created. They are arrogant, haughty, and dismissive of other people. They are certain that they are always right, and when they find out they're wrong, they will blame someone else for giving them misinformation or misleading them. Although they seem confident, the truth is that their self-esteem is unstable, and anything that truly brings them down can result in a profound depression.

Less Obvious Traits of Narcissism

The traits mentioned above are some of the more obvious traits of narcissistic personality disorder, but there are some characteristics that are not as obvious. Let's explore some of those.

- **Sometimes they're quiet and shy**: When you think about a narcissist, you likely think about someone who is loud and brash, and that's true for some, but there are some narcissists—the covert ones—who are the opposite. They are quiet and shy. They still feel the same way that loud ones feel, but they just don't show it in the same way. These narcissists will often even do good deeds, but the problem is that they are doing those good deeds for all the wrong reasons. They just want the accolades and recognition that comes from doing them. If they don't get that, they will often quietly harbor deep resentment.

- **Sometimes they fail**: Not all narcissists tell just victory stories. Though most narcissists are fond of telling stories about themselves, sometimes, instead of bragging about their many accomplishments, they tell stories of being victimized. They often do this with an air of entitlement that lets you know they believe they have been wronged and are deserving of much more. They will also frequently tell these kinds of stories with an attitude of self-reference. They will talk about how they are misunderstood or not properly recognized for all they have done. But, whether it's a story of accomplishment or failure, the important part is that it's still all about them.

- **They are status-oriented**: Most narcissists like nice things, but not in the same way that someone who is materialistic or a shopaholic likes nice things. They are concerned with the sense of status that the material objects in their life convey. They want to have the nice car and the big house so they can associate with other people of that same status and prove they are of high status too. That's how you can distinguish them from someone who is just materialistic. It's not the material that's important to the narcissist; it's the status it gives them.

- **You flatter them to pacify them**: If you find yourself flattering someone just to keep the peace, that's a red flag that they're a narcissist. Flattery works because you're giving the narcissist their narcissistic supply of adoration and admiration. That's what they crave because they are externally validated. They have no internal sense of self-esteem. They must get it from external sources, and thus, your flattery does the trick. If you find you do that frequently with someone in your life, and it works, you're likely dealing with a narcissist.

- **They live for the likes**: Social media is a narcissist's heaven, as long as they're getting those likes. Most narcissists love social media because they can project the image they want to and receive the external validation they so desperately need. They do everything they can to promote themselves as successful, attractive, and well-liked, so they will post their most attractive (and sometimes fake) photos online, seek out broader networks of "friends," and create posts that paint themselves in the best light possible, even if it means lying. This is all to garner the positive attention they need to prop up their self-image.

- **They don't have a clue**: Most narcissists have no idea they are narcissists. Since narcissism often originates in childhood, this is just the way the narcissist thinks everyone is. They have been socialized to believe they are a certain way and other people are not as good as they are. They have developed adaptive defense mechanisms as a result of a childhood where they were there to serve their parent's narcissism, or they were devalued and had to build up their own pathological defenses. No matter the specifics, they usually don't understand why people become annoyed at them. They don't know they have a problem because they have never had to look at themselves. Quite the opposite is true—they've often been forced to focus on other people their entire lives.

- **Most are men**: Men are almost twice as likely to have problems with NPD as women are, and the rates of narcissism in general are increasing, as we have seen. The fact that more narcissists are men is likely due to how boys are socialized in our society. They are praised for their assertiveness and desires for power, and these same traits are discouraged in girls.

What's more is that the difference in how children are treated begins at birth. As soon as people find out the biological sex of the child, they start to act one way with boys and another with girls. Boys are taught to be masculine by suppressing their emotions. Any feelings they might have of fear, sadness, or vulnerability are not acknowledged. These gender norms perpetuated on children at such early ages can lead to that child developing what is referred to as a "false self."

This mask protects the child from the vulnerable feelings that they have been taught to consider shameful or unmanly. It can get to the point that a man might not even be aware he has those kinds of feelings. He just feels ill-at-ease with understanding what's causing it.

Boys and men learn how to mask that kind of discomfort by doing manly things. They dominate others, bully them, exclaim their accomplishments loudly, and might even strive for comfortable and appropriate types of success like being the captain of the football team. These are things they feel comfortable with, and that's what they turn to when they are sensing the presence of more uncomfortable types of feelings.

All while they do this, they are feeling empty inside, perhaps even like a fraud. That's because they are disconnected from who they really are and the myriad feelings that come with being human.

Conclusion

Recognizing a narcissist is not always as easy as looking for the brash, boastful loudmouth in the room. There are nuances to their behavior that are easy to miss. Likewise, they are often very charming when making a first impression, and it isn't later that you will see a sudden and striking change in their behavior. By that time, you're often hooked on the person you initially thought was charming, maybe even the perfect partner for you. It's hard to admit that someone you thought you knew is not whom they seemed to be, and that can make it hard to take the steps you need to in order to protect yourself.

It's helpful to understand how the narcissist is feeling inside as all of this is happening. It can give you some insight into why they behave the way they do, which can later help you take the steps necessary to establish strong boundaries and ensure you're treated with respect. By knowing how they think, you can better understand and prepare for the actions they might take. This can help you develop strategies for improving your interactions and relationship with them. In the next chapter, we will examine how the narcissist thinks and feels as they are going through the various changes in behavior you're witnessing.

Chapter Seven: From Charm to Harm—How a Psychopathic Narcissist Thinks and Feels

"Narcissism is a grave condition of insecurity and desperately feeling unloved and unacceptable. An individual with Narcissistic Personality Disorder inherently believes they are 'damaged goods' and fears other individuals will discover the truth: that they feel powerless." —Melanie Tonia Evans

When you're involved with a narcissist, you see only one side of this disturbing mental disorder. To those who are subjected to the rage of a narcissist in their life, it appears that the only thing they think about is themselves. They are often boastful and seem very confident, but is that the reality of what is happening that way on the inside? It's helpful to hear from those who know they are narcissists.

Inside the Mind of a Narcissist

Carrie, a self-described narcissist, poignantly writes the following about her inner life when asked how a narcissist feels and thinks inside:

"Nervous.

Exhausted. Exhausted. Exhausted.

Self-fulfilled, but doomed to be alone.

Great on a day I have all my bases covered. But again, exhausted by then.

Tired. Alone.

Did I mention exhausted? Exhausted because I'm constantly making sure everything is in its place so my nasty web I need to survive has been woven correctly. And just right. And double checking and doing it again. Every detail. What you think, how I look, how I think you look, how you should look... Why the fuck you would do that that *way? Are you dumb? Must be.*

I'm thinking about how the aftermath with so-n-so is going to look. How the previous aftermath with this other so-n-so is playing out. Do I need to call them? Do they need a little more stringing along? I thought I put this other person on silent treatment?! They shouldn't be contacting me! This chick is important, how is she viewing me? What the fuck was that checker at the grocery store thinking that he could giggle and have lively conversation with me?! Eww, he needs to wash his nasty shirt before even thinking about talking to me. Even then, not worthy. I hope I was cold enough that I got my point across for him not to talk to me again. I hope he gets that he sucks.

How do I look to this obviously important guy over here in his sexy Corvette? Now how can I dump this loser I'm with... This person sucks. Did I say something to this important person this morning correctly? Wait, I'm the shit—I said it fine. Perfect. Is my hair right? Will this purse say anything about the status I'm trying to project? Yup, it looks good on me. I carry it so well. Because it's clearly obvious this is who I just naturally am; a SO important person who effortlessly carries this type of purse. Did they notice it? Duh, they did, and I made a lasting impression. How can I get out of banging my boyfriend tonight? I don't want him anymore and he repulses me. But I need him around a little longer, but he's not worthy. He doesn't get any. I'm too good now. I want him to think he's done something wrong. He has. He has because I'm done. That simple.

*Tip of the iceberg in my brain right there. This madness is ALWAYS. And more. This shit doesn't stop. I can't turn it off. I want to just **BE**. Why the fuck can't I just BE?!! How can I turn off this need to care what I think the whole world thinks?? Can I just wear a damn sweater with my hair up at my best friends house and chill and watch a damn movie?! And enjoy it?! Oh wait, that wouldn't work because I don't have any friends like that I can just chill with. Like I said, even if I did I couldn't anyways because I CAN'T JUST CHILL.*

Sooo yup, exhausted.

This is all day, every damn day. Every damn minute, every damn second. Constantly checking myself, always."

Arn describes his feelings as a narcissist after years of severe physical abuse at the hands of his mother:

"Of course, I thought I was normal. I didn't trust anyone. I always made sure I did and said whatever I had to to make anyone believe what I needed for them to do so, and I got what I needed or wanted. I had learned to lie better and make it sound like the truth by mixing in parts of the truth to a lie to make it true. I never did anything for nothing; I always made sure I was right and never wrong. If you were mean to me, I was gonna make you pay even worse than what you did to me. I learned I could talk to people with logic and common sense and make them believe what I wanted them to believe. I also learned that being honest most of the time let me get away with being dishonest or doing things without being suspected.

My development of these things was unstoppable, and I learned that apologizing was an easy way to get people to believe in you even more. I learned that I could be so charming and attentive to girls that it would make them feel good and special, and that they gave up a lot for that feeling. I still had that anger issue and would easily cut off family and friends if they upset me, and that was easy. I had some weird things like not connecting to people's problems of sadness or happiness or anything.

I hate hugging, I didn't like kissing. I never made love to my wife, it's always just been great sex. I would finish, ask her if she liked it, and put my clothes on and go to the living room.

All this was normal behavior. I never planned out anything, did things on purpose. I now think to myself: how could I have ever thought I was normal after all that abuse? I hardly have any family I speak to anymore or friends. What's crazy is that I would hate the people I was angry with. It happens at the time, it is while you're angry you can't control the anger, it's overwhelming and it's like something uncontrollable leaps out of you! I will be so angry and tell you things you deserve for doing whatever it was you did to me. I wouldn't care about what I was telling you or doing to you! You know why? Because you didn't care about me!

So if you didn't care about me, I'm definitely not caring about you! So no regret or remembering when you were nice or that you loved me, or that maybe you weren't feeling good or anything. All I know is you did or said something to fuck me up, and now I'm gonna give it to you worse!

I lie only if I really need to, but you will never know because I don't lie for trivial reasons, so you will already regard me as an honest person. To this day, I still tell people what they wanna hear or act in the way I need to for people to hear and see what they need to, so they believe what they need to. It's all done as just me—just as who I am. I don't do it to be malicious or mean."

Toxic Thoughts

The two general types of narcissism are grandiose and vulnerable narcissism, and although they manifest outwardly very differently, they share the same toxic thoughts and severe inner critic. One of the most toxic ways this occurs is in their propensity to constantly compare themselves to other people.

Grandiose narcissists express this comparison as the need to put other people down to prop themselves up. They consider that they are more deserving than anyone else, whereas the vulnerable narcissist believes they are being victimized by other people. They are often jealous of what other people have and desperate to have what their friends and neighbors have—it's a "keeping up with the Joneses" kind of scenario.

The reason for the comparisons is the result of needing to have their own sense of self buoyed by coming out on top. They need that perceived superiority as part of the external validation they require. As Carrie demonstrated in writing about her inner dialogue, that inner critic is always there—always picking away at the narcissist's fragile self-esteem and never letting them rest. If they don't come out on top, they have to finagle an explanation for that. That's when they often direct their inner critic at other people. They use it to explain—in a negative way—why those people got something that the narcissist did not.

Who is the Inner Critic?

If you gave your inner genius as much credence as your inner critic, you would be light years ahead of where you now stand.

Alan Cohen

That inner critic is a destructive way of thinking, which is typically formed from hurtful experiences that happened early in life and played a role in shaping one's sense of self, other people, and the world at large. It's a cruel internal voice that typically offers a negative commentary about various aspects of life. It frequently attacks, insults, and undermines people, though it can also help you soothe yourself and can be self-aggrandizing. With the latter, it works to put other people down and often causes you to be hostile toward, or suspicious of, others.

For narcissists specifically, the inner critic often directs its commentary at other people. This is done to prop up their fragile self-esteem. For them, to direct their inner critic at themselves would be something that they would have difficulty handling. Therefore, if a coworker is promoted and they are not, the inner critic tells them it's because he's a sycophant—a phony who got what the narcissist deserved by fooling or sucking up to the boss. The narcissist is victimized by the coworker's success and must find a justification for why they were rewarded. If a narcissist is interested in dating a particular person, they might tell themselves something like, "How would he even be interested in someone else," or, "I'm so much prettier than she is." Again, the narcissist is looking for a reason that will keep their self-esteem afloat for why someone else might have gotten what they wanted.

When they're not comparing themselves to a specific person for any reason, narcissists may still have thoughts that include general comparisons with other people. They may think, for example, "Why can't they see how great I am? I'm way better than any of these people." Other thoughts include things like, "They should listen to me. After all, it's my opinion that's the most important," or, "How dare they ignore me! They must be stupid. Can't they see I'm much more intelligent than that person?" The thoughts are comparative in nature, but it's clear that the narcissist, even while exclaiming their superiority, is always doing so in a precarious and almost desperate manner. It's evident they are striving to convince themselves of their worth more than they are trying to convince anyone else of their greatness or even rightness.

Because of their inner critic and need for external validation, the narcissist sees other people as mere extensions of themselves. They admire those whom they see as being on their level or higher in status than they are—though they often compete with them and even strive to take them down, since it will make them feel even greater. For those whom the narcissist sees as being lower on the totem pole, they detest them. They see them as only existing to serve the narcissist's needs. In short, other people are quickly sorted in the narcissist's mind with regard to how they might serve and prop up their carefully crafted image.

Are They Really Insecure, or Do They Believe the Inner Hype?

Experts debate whether narcissists are simply covering for a fragile self-esteem, or if they genuinely believe themselves to be superior to other people. Some argue they aren't actually insecure, and that they do really believe they are better than others. But others point to the profound depression they experience if they do fail. It's helpful to take a closer look at why the narcissist feels the need to listen to their inner critic, so what will happen if they ignore that voice? What will they feel if that happens?

Noted psychologist and Director of Research and Education at The Glendon Association, Dr. Lisa Firestone writes that the narcissists she has worked with have told her they don't feel okay unless they feel special. It's like the old adage, "go big or go home;" either they're great or they're nothing. They simply can't accept being like other people. They believed that they must be better.

This suggests that their sense of self is fragmented and that at some point in their life, they learned it wasn't okay just to be themselves. Their self-perception became distorted as a result, and though they began to feel superior, that superiority is very easily threatened, indicating that the feeling of being better than everyone else is baseless or not fully believed by the narcissist.

Firestone recounts the story of one patient who compared herself to every person in the room when she first walked in. As she examined that behavior, she realized that her mother was constantly comparing her to other girls and telling her that she was by far the prettiest. Her mother was essentially basing the child's value on the comparison with other people rather than on her inherent worth as a human being. She taught her daughter to do the same.

Research shows that many narcissists are produced by parental overvaluation rather than a lack of love or warmth. Self-esteem, on the other hand, is something that requires parental warmth for development, and it is not constructed in a healthy manner by parental overvaluation. In other words, if your parents are always comparing you to other children, even if they are comparing you favorably, it doesn't help to build up your self-esteem. Instead, it can result in feelings of superiority and entitlement. However, without an internally validated self-esteem, those grandiose feelings are merely a house of cards waiting to collapse when the day finally comes for you to learn that you are not the prettiest, most intelligent, or most successful person in that room.

Many times, parents will offer their child special treatment, build them up, or falsely praise them, not because they are conveying a genuine sense of love, warmth, or nurturance, but because they are compensating for a lack of those feelings toward that child. This is particularly true of narcissistic parents, and it produces narcissistic children. What a child needs to build a healthy self-esteem is genuine warmth, support, and acceptance of them and their value as a person.

So, the answer to the question posed is that a narcissist may, in fact, believe they are superior. They may buy into the hype, but when something happens to challenge that belief, they lack the solid foundation of a genuine sense of self-worth to sustain it. That often results in profound depression as they strive to deal with the conflicting emotions that inevitably arise.

Narcissistic Behaviors— "Manipulationships"

The inner, toxic thinking of the narcissist, as you might imagine, results in some pretty abusive behavior toward the people in their life. They are such master manipulators that some people refer to relationships with a narcissist as "manipulationships." To deal with this, it's helpful to understand the manipulative tactics that a narcissist uses. We'll go over them briefly here, though they will be covered in more detail in the second book in this set. Here are a few manipulative behaviors and some general guidelines for how to handle them.

- **Verbal Abuse**: This can take many forms, but typically involves blaming, shaming, and devaluing you. The goal is to shame you into falling in line with the behavior they want from you. When this kind of treatment begins, the best thing you can do is walk away. Let the narcissist know that you'll be happy to have a calm discussion with them when they can do so respectfully.

- **Gaslighting**: This is a very common tactic that narcissists use to make you doubt your own perception of reality. They will flat out deny that something happened when you know it did, tell you they didn't mean it the way you took it, or say you're just overly sensitive. Trust your gut here because you can easily begin to wonder if it happened the way you think it did. It can also help to document interactions you have with them right after it has happened.

- **Deception/Lying**: This is another go-to tool for the narcissist. They will lie regularly without compunction. Remember that to lose control of a situation is something they see as extremely threatening to their carefully crafted image. You can't necessarily know they are lying, but know that they will, and double check anything that doesn't sound right.

- **Emotional Blackmail**: Again, because the narcissist is so focused on projecting a certain image, if you threaten that in some way, they will use anything they can to make you feel as though you must do something to make it up to them. They will also try to make you feel guilty as if you owe them. If you give into this kind of tactic, the narcissist will use it again and again.

- **Competition**: Because the narcissist believes themselves to be superior, they will get very competitive in order to prove that fact. They will compete with anyone. Narcissistic parents will even compete with their own children. They believe they must prove themselves, and they feel they must crush you in order to do so. The best thing you can do here is simply to refuse to compete with them. Just do what you need to do for yourself, not out of competition.

- **Comparison**: Narcissists will compare you to themselves or someone else, and you won't come out on top. They are constantly negatively comparing the people in their life to other people. It's part of proving they are superior and devaluing others to keep them in line. To combat this tactic, you have to work on knowing your own worth and refusing to buy into the comparison.

- **Withholding**: Narcissists can be withholding in many ways. It might involve emotional or financial withholding. They might refuse to give you something you need or share something with you. They can even withhold things like communication, and they will often refuse to give you what you want or need unless and until you do what they want. If they have something you want or need, the best thing you can do is look elsewhere, but that won't always be possible. Another tactic is to comply with their wishes, but you might not want or be able to do that. The only option you may ultimately be left with is to remove yourself from the relationship until the narcissist can agree to compromise with you.

- **Sabotage**: Narcissists are so desperate to ensure that they are seen as superior that they will use any technique they can to make sure their carefully crafted image is maintained. That includes sabotage. They may sabotage your work or your relationships. They will stop at nothing to ensure their image is safe. This is another tactic that you simply have to be aware of and look out for when dealing with a narcissist. If you're at work, document everything you do with witnesses if possible. If they are attempting to sabotage a relationship you have, you might need to talk to the other person and let them know there's a problem.

- **Neglect**: This is often the case with narcissistic parents. They are so focused on their own needs and desires that they simply can't see the needs of others, including their own children. Since they can't empathize with other people, they are not capable of understanding what they are going through, and thus, it's easy for them to become neglectful. It's something to be aware of and check on if the narcissist in your life has children.

- **Boundary Crossing**: Narcissists see you as an extension of themselves, and thus, they don't understand that you have boundaries. They believe they should be able to simply do what they want without even thinking about it, let alone asking your permission. To defend against this tactic, you'll need to set and maintain strong boundaries with consistent, well-enforced consequences for crossing them.

- **Isolation**: Narcissists will definitely seek to isolate you from friends and family. They don't want you to have a support system to turn to because it will make it easier for you to see their manipulations. This is something you don't want to allow. You need to have and maintain contact with a strong support network of people whom you can turn to when needed.

- **Financial Abuse**: Narcissists will definitely try to control you through financial domination or by leaving you without any resources. They might even steal from you or accrue debt in your name. You need to maintain control over your own finances to keep this from happening.

- **Violence**: Narcissists are not above using violence as a way to manipulate your behavior. Of course, not all narcissists are violent, and not all physically abusive people are narcissists, but it's a relatively common tactic for narcissists. The physical abuse can take the form of beatings, but it can also involve blocking you from moving around or going where you want. They might also destroy your property or throw things at you. You should not tolerate violence in any form. It will only get worse, so if this starts, you should get yourself to someplace safe once you can do so safely.

Trauma Bonding

Trauma bonding refers to the survival strategy used by people in abusive relationships where they begin to feel trust and genuine affection for the person abusing them. Within the context of a relationship with a narcissist, it typically occurs when the narcissist's partner has problems with codependency. That's where they enable the behaviors of their partner.

If you are codependent, as your relationship with the narcissist begins to change, you'll see it happening, but you won't necessarily understand why. I know that was the case in my situation. I could see he was changing, but I didn't understand why, and at first, I enabled his behavior by making excuses for him.

A common thing that happens with the trauma bonded, codependent partner of a narcissist, however, is not just that they don't understand why this sudden change is occuring, but they also believe themselves to be responsible somehow. They feel that if they can just figure out what it is they are doing wrong, their loving partner will return to them. Like the abuser, the trauma bonded partner blames themselves for the problem.

The trauma bond is strengthened when the codependent partner looks to the narcissist for approval, love, and recognition. The problem with that is that the narcissist will surely escalate the abuse, since all they have to do to win you back is start showing you love again. Love should not be conditioned upon approval, and in the end, the narcissist cannot approve of anyone other than themselves.

Can a Narcissist Break Free of the Pattern?

The first challenge to breaking free of this toxic pattern of thinking is to recognize that it is actually toxic, and it's not what everyone else is going through. When you grow up in a particular environment, it often takes something traumatising - or a series of traumatic events - to make you realize that not everyone experiences reality like you do. For someone who is conditioned to believe they are superior to other people, that can take a long time and it may never happen.

If a narcissist does come to the realization that they have a problem and seeks to change their behavior, the best way to start is to challenge that inner critic. They have to recognize the pattern for when it begins its commentary, and then they have to start challenging what it is saying. This can help them understand that this is a habitual routine rather than their genuine point of view.

They begin this process by simply noticing when their inner voice starts piping up and when it takes a break. Once they have become adept at noticing it, they can start to counter what it's saying with more realistic and compassionate perspectives about other people and about themselves as well. As they start challenging that inner critic, they can begin exploring where it comes from, and perhaps, who it sounds like from their past. They can question the validity of their own self-esteem by exploring what happens to their sense of self if they try refuting what their inner voice is saying. What kind of emotions arise when they do that? Do they find it threatening to challenge that inner voice?

Once they've started exploring the origins of their inner critic, they can work to heal old traumas, which will help them oppose the directives of that inner critic. As they do this difficult work, they will develop a stronger sense of self-compassion. This is probably the strongest antidote for narcissism. Self-compassion isn't based on self-evaluation; rather, it's learning to treat yourself as you would treat your best friend. It's understanding that you're human and can make mistakes, but that doesn't mean you don't have value. It's being kind to yourself, just as you are kind to your best friend.

Moreover, self-compassion involves taking a mindful approach to your own thoughts and feelings, being aware of what you're thinking and why. It also means not becoming overly-identified with those thoughts and not getting too attached to them, but simply being curious about them and letting them pass. You don't have to buy into the story the inner critic is spinning. You don't have to go down the rabbit hole of destructive thoughts, endless comparison to others, and devaluation of yourself and those you love. You can choose simply to notice these thoughts, and then let them pass.

Finally, the narcissist can learn to accept the common humanity of all people. This can be difficult because it means recognizing that you're not different or special, or better said, not any more different or special than anyone else. Everyone has inherent worth as a human being. It's not a binary choice between either being special or being nothing. You can be an ordinary, wonderful person, but this is often a very difficult pattern for the narcissist to break. They have spent their entire lives in nearly constant comparison with almost everyone around them. They've had precious little rest from their destructive inner critic, and once they start to explore the reasons behind their actions, that reality can be very painful.

Conclusion

Narcissism is the result of a toxic childhood environment in which the narcissist was not helped in constructing a solid foundation of self-worth. Instead, they were subjected to emotional, and sometimes physical, abuse that created a pattern of inner critic commentary, which negatively assesses each and every detail of their life. It's a truly nightmarish inner world where they must question every decision, compare it to everyone around them, and if they are criticized for their choices, they often spiral into deep depression because they lack a true sense of self-worth.

From this perspective, it's easy to see why they behave the way they do and why it's so difficult for them to escape this way of thinking. The devaluation of others can be understood in terms of the need to be on top constantly. Although they might genuinely believe in their superiority, they are thrown into self-doubt by the most minor perceived slight. What would be a constructive suggestion to you is a slap in the face to a narcissist. They believe that the fault must lie with others because narcissists lack the internal self-worth to realize that even if the fault is theirs, they still have value. It's a sad, tragic reality and one that leaves them with many fears. That's what we'll examine in the next chapter: the fears they have and why.

Chapter Eight: **What Narcissists Fear the Most and Why They are Like That**

"When I look at narcissism through the vulnerability lens, I see the shame-based fear of being ordinary. I see the fear of never feeling extraordinary enough to be noticed, to be lovable, to belong, or to cultivate a sense of purpose." —Brené Brown

It can't be easy trying to always keep up the appearance of perfection, find excuses for any flaws or failures along the way, and prompt external validation that is the only life raft for your self-esteem. Living like that has to create a lot of fear. After all, you might get exposed at any moment by something out of your control, and many things are out of your control. What's worse is that you might have to face yourself, look into the depths of your pain, and see the reality that your illusion is creating abuse. When you think about how the narcissist thinks, you can have compassion for their fears. But what exactly do they fear?

From the Trenches...

Phillip, who loved a narcissist, writes:

"Narcissists hate themselves the most. Narcissists fear themselves the most. They don't fear you, they need you. They fear another minute sitting alone in a quiet room with nothing to hear but their own empty thoughts, and they hate what they will do to avoid it. They do not like who they are. When they look in the mirror, they see a menace.

It doesn't matter how beautiful you think the narcissist is, your love will never be a match for the hatred they feel for themselves. Narcissists are full of fear. They are afraid of everything, but the thing they fear the most is the same exact thing that they hate: themselves.

The closer you get to them, the closer they have to look at themselves, and that they cannot do. Of course, they fear exposure, they fear not being good enough, they fear failure, they fear rejection, they fear life. They fear you because you know them, but what they really fear is the person they wake up to every single day: themselves. That is the thing that they hate the most. The man (or woman) in the mirror.

Every single moment of a narcissist's life will be spent avoiding that one thing because it is the only thing that they cannot manipulate or lie to. It is with them every single second of every single day. That is a day in hell for them. A day spent looking in the mirror without an escape."

Pedro agrees when he writes:

"Themselves.

Rather, the part of themselves that comprises their toxic conscience: their superego.

The part of themselves that represents the abusive early caretakers that planted the seeds of their narcissism and made them blossom through psychological abuse, thereby setting the tone for the narcissistically disordered way of being that makes that person grow to become just like those whom they once hated and feared the most... and naturally loving too, because they don't know better.

A self-perpetuating prophecy of personal doom, carried along across bloodlines immemorial, as though it were a poisoned Kool-aid chalice that the child is made to drink in the guise of toxic education."

And this from Amy, a self-described curious human with compassion, who writes:

"Being seen. They fight the fear of discovery with every breath. They inhale fear and exhale lies. I can't imagine how exhausting. I do remember the pain of the lies and cruelty."

> Narcissists live their lives in constant fear. What do they fear most? Every single thing they did to you that caused suffering. They fear being: abandoned, controlled, criticized, smeared and exposed— to you, the world, but even worse, themselves.

What Do the Experts Say?

We've seen how the illusion is constructed and how a child is taught to feel entitled and superior but isn't taught how to know their true value. It results in a person who pretends. They pretend they are omnipotent, omniscient, and that nothing can touch them. They are superior to everyone else, deserve and are entitled to special treatment, and if they don't get it, fly into a rage. That's how they act, but their actions are born of fear.

Behind their house of cards lies a weak foundation, one in which they are dependent on external validation constantly propping up their fragile self-esteem. What's worse, they don't really know that; they just know they are always on edge and fearful of being exposed. That makes them vulnerable to even the slightest and most gentle of criticism. Moreover, they have many fears because deep down, they know something is wrong. Here are some of the fears that experts have identified through their research.

1. **Relationship Commitment**

   Most narcissists have extreme difficulty with establishing and maintaining lasting, meaningful relationships. When you remember how they are made, think, and feel, you can understand why this would be difficult for them. To be in an intimate relationship with someone, you have to be willing to be vulnerable and let your guard down.

   This is what the narcissist really fears, since that means their partner will see them for who they really are, and the truth is, they don't even know who they really are. Their entire self-image is a carefully crafted construction based on false premises. They lie about their abilities to impress people and get the admiration they need, they pursue materialistic things to appear more successful than they are, and they boast about abilities they don't really have, so they can receive accolades for things they never did.

   Of course, they fear that someone will get close enough to see the truth. That's why they have to keep any potential romantic partners on edge. They believe they must break them down, so their partner won't look too closely at the narcissist. They'll be too busy looking at themselves.

2. Going Deep

Because their sense of self is little more than a facade they've been creating their entire life, narcissists fear examining their own psyche. They don't want to discover their inadequacies, flaws, or that they are merely human. They have spent a great deal of time convincing themselves that they are superior and entitled to special treatment.

If they delve too deeply into personal growth work, they risk learning the truth: that they are just like everyone else and vulnerable. For a narcissist, that is a life-shattering realization. That's why they must find fault with others constantly, so they won't have to look at their own failings. If you imagine this is your reality, what steps would you take to avoid learning the truth? Would you gaslight your lover? Would you lie to your boss? Would you push your own children away? Of course, you would.

3. Criticism

Narcissists can't stand being even gently criticized, let alone insulted. They are hypersensitive because they fear being exposed as a fraud. For that reason, they experience the pain of an insult much more than most people. Narcissists feel it as a crushing blow and something that must be avenged. They will seek revenge against someone they perceive as having been critical of them. They must crush the criticism before someone looks more deeply—possibly even the narcissist themselves—and discovers that they are human after all.

That hypersensitivity makes them hypervigilant to any and all perceived insults or criticism. They even become paranoid and often take preemptive steps to cut their critics off at the pass, as it were. They will often take their critics down before they even say anything. That's why they will act condescending and superior, even before any criticism has been mentioned.

4. Shame

Another big fear that most narcissists have is a shame. Remember that their self-image is based wholly on their status in society and how they are thought of by other people. Most work hard to create an image of someone who should be held in high regard. Thus, if they are subjected to shame, that image is at risk. Interestingly, although they fear shame, they don't fear feeling guilty. Guilt would mean they felt badly about doing or saying something they should not have, but how can they have done something wrong if they are superior?

Since narcissists lack empathy, they are incapable of putting themselves in other people's shoes. That means they can't feel guilty because they can't see that they have done something to hurt someone else. However they can feel shame, particularly if they are singled out by their friends or community for something they said or did and that threatens their status. This is something that can hurt the narcissist, and it is something they will take great pains to avoid. That's why they'll frequently blame others for their mistakes, and if it looks like that won't work, they'll misdirect the criticism with gaslighting. That's where they'll simply lie to convince you that what you experienced isn't what you think you experienced.

5. Lack of Admiration

Narcissists must get their narcissistic supply from people outside of themselves. They feed on admiration and adoration from other people, and without that, they believe they are nothing. Their self-worth is entirely externally validated. They don't have the inner capacity to value themselves simply as humans. They need the adoration and admiration of others to prop up their sense of self. Without it, they have no value.

That's why ignoring a narcissist is one of the worst things you can do to them. It makes them feel irrelevant and unimportant; in other words, they feel totally worthless. This is why they can be extremely charming at first and when they believe they have gone too far and might lose your admiration forever. That charm, however, is often short-lived, and it is all too frequently replaced with rage.

6. **Being Seen as Unimportant**

Narcissists will often pursue positions of power and influence so that they can get that external validation they so desperately need. That's why it's not surprising that many tyrants are or were narcissists. They need the power to prop up their sense of self-worth, but they usually don't want to do what it takes to deserve the power and be beloved by the people over whom they have power. They just want the admiration that comes with that power.

Additionally, narcissists are very competitive; they want to win. Being a leader is the ultimate victory, and it makes them feel good about themselves. It's usually very short-lived, however, and they don't want to do the work it takes to maintain that sense of greatness. It's often not long before they are criticized for their failures, and that's when their rage emerges, usually with tragic consequences.

7. Getting Caught in a Lie

As we've seen, narcissists lie regularly, and it plays an important role in helping them maintain the carefully crafted image they present to the world. That's why they live in fear of being found out. If someone can expose them as a liar, their entire self-image is at risk. They fear the world will see them for the weak, insecure person they really are. You might think that would make them more truthful, but they just can't do it because they have to create that image. It means they must at least stretch the truth, and when they start doing that, they become paranoid that someone might find out about their lies.

8. Feeling Remorse

The problem with a narcissist is not that they are incapable of feeling remorse; it's that they actively refuse to show any remorse for anything they have done. Remorse is equal to weakness in their mind, and they believe that you could show yourself as vulnerable if you show any kind of weakness. Showing remorse would also mean they are admitting they made a mistake, and that is something that they are loath to do.

9. Feeling Gratitude

Like remorse, gratitude in the mind of a narcissist is equivalent to weakness. It's also an acknowledgment that someone did something for you that was helpful or that you could not do for yourself. It means you owe someone, and narcissists simply can't accept that. They believe themselves to be all-knowing, always in the right, and even omnipotent—Greenberg's GOD designation—thus, to need something from someone else or to be indebted to someone else is not something they can allow. It makes them feel weak and needy, and that is a threat to their image, and internally, to their self-esteem.

10. Being Alone

This is a huge fear for the narcissist since it means they must sit with themselves. Their self-esteem is externally validated, and that's why they like to have people around them at all times, adoring and admiring them. Without those people, they must try to prop themselves up, and that's not something they can do because of the self-loathing and shame they feel. When alone, they feel a profound sense of loneliness, and they fear it will never let up. That's why they are terrified of being alone and lonely.

11. Aging and Death

Of course, narcissists are not the only people who fear getting older and dying, but for the narcissist, it is an exaggerated fear. They have built themselves up to be superior beings, and old age and death are the only things they cannot beat. It destroys even the most powerful among us, but for the narcissist, that fact makes them just like everyone else: mortal. Many narcissists will even refuse to accept that they are going to die because it would mean that all they've tried to do has been pointless.

Conclusion

Narcissists like to pretend that nothing scares them, but the reality is that they are full of fear. After I left my ex-husband, I realized the depth of his fear as he tried so many different ways to get me back. When you see how desperate narcissists are to keep you in their life, you realize they are not as confident and fearless as they would like you to believe. When you understand that they have spent an enormous amount of time creating an image that they need so that people will validate them, you can understand the reason for many of the fears listed above. When you live in a house of cards, you are constantly afraid of any kind of breeze that might bring the whole thing down. That fear makes you willing to do a lot of things to maintain that image. It's a vicious cycle that the narcissist cannot escape.

We've been exploring the narcissist's point of view and how this devastating mental condition develops, but you might also be wondering why you attracted a narcissist in the first place. Maybe it's not even your first one. That can really make you think that there's something about you—some flaw that's drawing them in or weakness they're seeing in you. The reality is much different, however, and that's what we'll examine in the next chapter.

Chapter Nine: Empaths, Success Stories, and Other Types that Attract Narcissists

"Nice people don't necessarily fall in love with nice people." —Jonathan Franzen.

When my ex-husband started revealing his true self to me, I was confused, frightened, and began to doubt myself. I didn't understand what was going on, but I did notice certain patterns of behavior in our relationship. One thing I noticed was that he definitely felt that I increased his status among his peers. He wanted me on his arm so he could show me off to his friends and business colleagues. Before I even realized he was a narcissist, I understood that he was using me to show everyone how great he was; he must be to get someone as beautiful and intelligent as me. The thing was that he didn't truly appreciate my qualities; he simply used them to improve his standing in the world. I would later come to find out that such was typical of narcissists. Let's hear some other stories.

Why Do I Attract Narcissists?

Many people wonder why they seem to attract one narcissist after another. Let's look at why many think that is.

Lin, who survived six narcissists, writes:

"In my opinion, narcissists do not seek any specific type of woman. The woman is irrelevant; she is nothing more than a tool to use in their quest to get the things they desire in life.

If he or she (in case the narcissist is a lesbian) finds a woman who is needy, with low self-esteem, that's a plus. Alcoholics, even better. A slut, you betcha. Game on. But wait, if she is that easy to manipulate, the narcissist won't need to bring much of their game to the relationship, and that isn't any fun.

Unfortunately, it doesn't take a narcissist long to use up someone like that. It's almost too easy for a master manipulator, and they will chew her up and spit her out quickly. UNLESS...

She has money or status.

That is and always will be the determining factor in who the narcissist chooses as their primary supply. Because the narcissist has needs; great big luxurious needs that they think they deserve, and if they can find one who will satisfy those needs, the most beautiful woman in the world won't stand a chance in their eyes.

If you have money and will buy the narcissist anything they want, they are yours. Forever. Or until you run out of money. Here is a list of the female attributes that are trumped by wealth:

1. *BEAUTY*
2. *AGE*
3. *SEXINESS*
4. *INTERESTING JOB*
5. *INTELLIGENCE*
6. *CREATIVITY*
7. *42DDD BOOBS*
8. *NICE CAR*
9. *NICE HOUSE*
10. *GREAT PERSONALITY*

Bottom line is that YOU don't matter. You, as a person or a woman, are irrelevant. You will have no more importance to them than their trimmer. The only thing a narcissist is looking for is someone who will make their lives better."

Virginia, who had relationships with three narcissists, writes the following:

"All three of the NPDs I was involved with for over two years stated how they loved my traits—even during breakups they mentioned my traits.

They want strong, independent, smart women. They like hard-working, goal-oriented women, women who are resilient, flexible, yet decisive. They like women who are great listeners. There are more traits than this, but you get the jist of it.

They DON'T like weakness at all. They don't like weak women. They may use weak women, but they are not attracted to them. Narcissists want to be associated with women who make them look better, who have the resources and social skills that they lack. The narcissists I knew liked the fact that I am self-directed/motivated. I don't need to be cheered on or motivated or instructed on how to plan my life. I get up daily, knowing what I will do.

I was with two cerebral narcissists, and this is what they liked. BUT, at some point, all of your positive traits end up threatening the narcissist's ability to manipulate and control you. If you are a few steps ahead of them, and you know what they are, you will soon be in the doghouse! No kind of woman will be liked for too long before the narcissist becomes jealous of your fine traits. He begins to see you as his competition. Get ready to be devalued. The narcissist will never accept losing or being second best."

Finally, Boaz, who was married for 28 years to a narcissist, writes:

"A narcissist needs someone that strokes their emotional ego or gives them something that they are in need of. The three types of people that narcissists are attracted to are:

- ***The empath** or **codependent**—Someone who has an innate desire to help and feel deeply.*

- ***The obsessed**—Someone who feeds into their ego because they have a particular obsession with them. It could be race, skin color, gender-based, or something else. This will keep the mate from seeing who the narcissist really is.*

- *The perfect broken person*—This is someone that has everything in check. A person of power, someone making good money, someone who is extremely attractive. However, there is always one hitch—this person has to have a very apparent weakness as well. The narcissist will use this against them any chance they get."

What Do the Experts Say?

Whenever you're experiencing a breakup, it's natural to ask yourself what went wrong and what role you played. People who get out of relationships with narcissists can be particularly hard on themselves because they feel like they allowed the abuse to go on too long before leaving. When they come to understand that their ex was a narcissist, they might recognize that it's been a pattern with them, and of course, they want to know what it is about them that attracts this kind of abuser.

If you're wondering why you seem to attract narcissists, you might wonder if you're simply weak or easy to manipulate, but you might be surprised to learn that this isn't the case at all. As we've seen, narcissists need adoration, admiration, and almost constant external validation. Their self-esteem is very fragile, and if the people around them have a different opinion from theirs, they will frequently see this as criticism. When they're criticized, they usually seek to punish their critic.

What's more, narcissists are very concerned about their image. They value their appearance and perceived success. It doesn't really matter if they're simply riding the coattails of other, more successful people; they have convinced themselves they are entitled to that. They believe, in fact, that they deserve to have the very best of everything life has to offer.

Because of these characteristics, there are certain personality traits that will tend to attract these kinds of toxic, emotionally abusive people. Let's explore the various types of people that most often attract narcissists.

1. **Caretakers**

   People with caretaking personalities—*givers*—often attract narcissists because it suits their sense of entitlement perfectly. These kinds of people like to help others, and they are frequently self-sacrificing. That's just what the narcissist is looking for because they believe that they are deserving of everything someone wants to give them. They believe this because they think of themselves as special and superior to others. The problem is that they don't appreciate the giving nature of those natural caretakers. In fact, they feel as though their partner is lucky to be in a relationship with them, so there is no need for gratitude or appreciation.

2. **Empaths and People with Forgiving Natures**

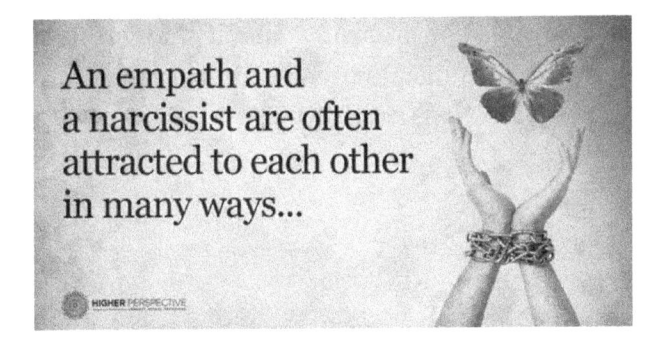

An empath and a narcissist are often attracted to each other in many ways...

HIGHER PERSPECTIVE

You might find this surprising because narcissists lack empathy, but they do, in fact, seek out people who are very empathic. Empaths are people who want to help others, and they also have the ability to sense the emotional fragility that is part of the narcissist's inner life. They want to help the narcissist, to heal them. Unfortunately, the narcissist sees their empathy as something they can take advantage of to get their narcissistic supply of attention and external validation.

When a narcissist recognizes that someone is an empath, they will often be sure to relate personal stories of tragedy and abuse they have suffered to gain sympathy. They will also use those stories as an excuse for their bad behavior. If you're an empath or forgiving person, you might understand why such past treatment could make the narcissist behave like they do. The problem is that it's not a solution to prevent their abusive treatment of you.

3. Successful People

This might be another surprising category of people for attracting narcissists, but when you remember that the narcissist is all about creating a certain image and maintaining a high status, you can understand how someone like this can help. For this reason, narcissists will often befriend or choose romantic partners that enhance their status. Here, there are two categories of narcissists to consider.

Somatic narcissists are obsessed with their appearance. They strive to maintain a youthful, attractive external appearance. They frequent the gym and spend a lot of time in front of mirrors. Because of their obsession with appearance, they will typically focus on romantic partners that are physically attractive. They can see in their mind's eye the two of them out together being admired as a "sexy couple."

Cerebral narcissists, on the other hand, are those who consider themselves to be the most intelligent person in the room—the know-it-alls. They want to impress everyone with their many accomplishments and powerful positions. They would be more interested in a romantic partner who is educated and has a certain level of social status.

The problem with both of these types of narcissists is that they don't want their partner to outshine them. They want them to enhance their status, but they don't really want someone who tops them in any way, or worse, who might question or undermine their superiority. They really want their romantic partners to be "trophies," someone they can show off as if they were property in order to make themselves look good.

4. Easygoing People

Another trait we've discussed of narcissists is the need to always be right and win. Losing means you're a loser, and that's not something the narcissist can tolerate. That's why they like easygoing people. They need to keep the people around them in line so they won't jeopardize their image at all. They need them, in essence, to be obedient and agree with their rigid views. They use a lot of tactics to make that happen, but it's helpful to them if the people around them are more interested in maintaining harmony than expressing their own opinions or getting their way.

People who are natural peacemakers tend to compromise rather than continue fighting, and that's what the narcissist wants. Someone like this may not ask a lot of questions when the narcissist uses gaslighting to misdirect them, and they typically won't challenge the narcissist's worldview. In sum, they pose little threat to the narcissist's image.

5. Good-hearted People Who Look for the Best in Others

Someone who genuinely believes that most people are essentially good are perfect for the narcissist. This kind of person is hesitant to leave when the going gets tough. They would rather work things out, and they tend to project their own goodness onto their partner. It is often very painful and difficult for this type of person to change their worldview to accept that not everyone has the same good heart that they do, but until they realize that their narcissistic partner doesn't actually have their best interests at heart, they will continue to suffer from the abuse.

Conclusion

As you can see, it isn't the flaws in those whom narcissists are attracted to; rather, it is often their positive qualities. People who are intelligent, successful, empathic, friendly and good-hearted all have qualities that narcissists will exploit. My ex-husband exploited my physical beauty and success because those qualities made him look good to his friends and colleagues.

These are not, however, qualities that you should seek to change in yourself. Rather, you must try to protect them. Often, this means leaving the narcissist in your life, but if not, you'll need to learn strategies to protect yourself from their exploitation and emotional abuse. If you choose to leave them, you'll want to check out my second book, *FREE YOURSELF! A Complex PTSD Recovery Workbook for Women: 10 Steps to Go from Emotional Abuse Recovery to Building Healthy Relationships*, which can help you heal from the narcissistic abuse you've suffered and rebuild your life.

If you choose to stay with them, you'll want to read the second book in this set, which will give you strategies for protecting yourself from their abuse so you can live your best life, even with a narcissist. Before you make that decision, let's explore the question of whether or not a narcissist can truly love you.

Chapter Ten: **Can an Egotistical Toxic Person Truly Love You?**

"The lion is most handsome when looking for food." —Rumi

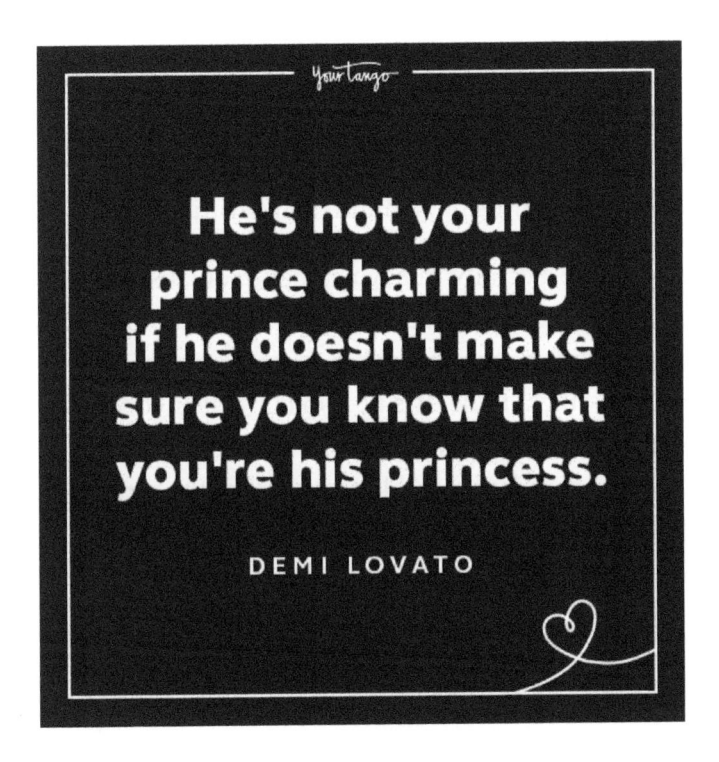

> He's not your prince charming if he doesn't make sure you know that you're his princess.
>
> — DEMI LOVATO

One of the things that was so painful to me after I left my ex-husband was wondering if he had ever loved me at all. There was such a sense of betrayal because of the image he had projected at the start of our relationship. That's part of why I would explain away his behavior as him having a bad day or that he's under stress—the typical excuses. It paralyzed me for a while, and that's typical of a relationship with a narcissist. You're often torn between the love you feel for this person and the pain they continuously cause you; you can't decide between staying with them or leaving. It's confusing, painful, and frustrating.

That's especially true when they vacillate between that caring, charming person you first came to know and love, and the unpredictable, often cruel person you now know them to be. It's no wonder that anyone who has ever had a relationship with a narcissist might ask, *"Did they ever love me?"* Let's see what the survivors say.

From the Trenches…

Angela writes the following:

"The biggest hurdle for a narcissist in loving another person is their inability to identify what another person is. Narcissists live in a world of mirrors. They cannot see you. They see a mirror. How can they love someone they cannot see? That being said, they can feel an attachment to you, a fondness, a liking, infatuation, even caring.

But all of these feelings are what they feel for the mirror that you are. And sadly, because of their fundamental shame, they will always eventually see the self-hatred they have for themselves reflected back from you. The wonderful, exhilarating, validating feelings you once gave them for themselves will always crumble when they are reminded that they feel no self-worth. When they looked at you, for a time, they were looking into a mirror, and they liked what they saw. Then one day, for some reason, they looked into that mirror that had made them feel so good, and they saw the 'truth' reflected back.

Narcissists can feel love—or what feels like love to them—but they can never really see you. They can feel love for you, but it is an illusion. It is love they feel for the reflection that they believe you are. They can only see themselves. And you can never stay a perfect reflection to someone that cannot believe they have any true worth."

Sophie, who has a Masters degree in psychology from the University of Toronto, writes:

"They don't love the way a healthy human being loves. It's a conditional and fickle kind of love. It's graded on the quality of the high our feelings for them create inside of them. The higher we make them feel, the higher quality supply we are to them. The greater the supply, the more they become infatuated with us. This is love to them.

Real love can't be turned off and on. Mature love will weather a storm. Two people in love will join forces... become a team, and will have one another's back. We build each other up and avoid hurting the one we love at all costs. The narcissistic love dissipates when they no longer feel the 'high' of the new relationship.

It is not love when a person can jump from relationship to relationship, causing massive amounts of pain in the other. That's not mature love."

Kate, a narcissist, writes the following:

"I think what I want most out of a relationship is to be saved. I used to think that I longed to find someone I could love back, but now I know it's a lot more shallow than that. Truth is, I was always just looking for someone to adore me hard enough that I could somehow see myself through their eyes. I wanted someone to mirror back my idealized self so that I could fall in love with my reflection too.

Ironically, relationships always bring out the worst in my personality. How am I supposed to love the screaming, distorted image glaring back? The problem is that I've never once thought about making someone else happy. It feels weird to admit it out loud, but I do not care about anyone else's feelings, not really.

Love bombing is never for the other person's benefit; it's designed to make them fall for you. It's strange to know that I've probably never done a kind thing for anyone that wasn't for my own gain. That's where I always go wrong."

How Do Narcissists Love?

Although most narcissists can show passion early on in a relationship, that usually doesn't last very long. As Kate suggested above, it's really about looking to love themselves more than looking to love another person. The initial high of a new relationship fuels their egoistic needs for a while, but for most narcissists, their relationships are transactional. They are playing games, and they are playing to win.

While they perceive, express, understand and manage emotions, they use these abilities to manipulate people so they can get them to love and admire them, thus helping them receive their narcissistic supply. They use a variety of techniques to seduce and impress you early on, and they can certainly make a great first impression. They can be adept at making love, and this can win them many conquests. They also use love bombing to overwhelm their partners with their expression of love for them.

Although all of this can win them your love, as the intimacy in the relationship increases, the narcissist typically loses interest. They are unable to sustain most relationships for more than six months to a few years. That's because the more intimate you are, the more likely you are to discover the truth about them—that is, their vulnerability. This causes them to prioritize power in a relationship over intimacy, and of course, as we've seen, they loathe vulnerability because they equate it with weakness.

As a relationship progresses, they prefer to use dominance and superiority to maintain control while avoiding genuine intimacy. They use games to get their needs met, and they also always keep their options open by flirting with other people and even cheating on their partner. Although the narcissist may develop genuinely positive feelings for their partner, those are usually based on friendship and shared interests rather than romantic intimacy.

When they marry, they typically change pretty quickly to someone who is cold, excessively critical, and full of rage, particularly if you dare to challenge them or refuse to give them what they want. They will usually only support your needs if it is something that is convenient for them and/or satisfying to their ego. When you disappoint them—and you will—they will quickly turn to devaluation, and they start looking elsewhere for someone who will prop up their self-esteem.

For partners who leave the narcissist, they usually feel bewildered by what just happened to them. I know I did. I couldn't understand how he changed from such a charming, seemingly wonderful man to a cold, angry man-child. I did feel crushed, utterly confused, discarded, and betrayed. It was a very low moment in my life when I realized that everything he presented to me was nothing more than a seductive veneer—a facade designed to lure me in for his own benefit. He didn't seem to feel love for me at all.

Narcissistic Love

Aristotle and St. Thomas Aquinas defined love as "to will the good of another." Others have described it as the union of two people, a union that necessitates that each see the other as a separate person. When you love someone, you are motivated by their needs, wants, and feelings, and you desire to give them encouragement and support. In short, you take pleasure from their happiness. The last thing you want to do is hurt them.

With mature love, you are concerned about the other person—you want to help them live their best life, and you support their personal growth. You want to know and understand their experience and worldview, even if it is different from your own. You give them your attention, respect, compassion, support, and above all, acceptance. This requires time and discipline, and you have to want to know and understand them. That's what creates a problem for the narcissist.

Narcissists lack empathy, which makes them unwilling to examine and understand the feelings and needs of other people. Some research suggests that this is due in part to structural abnormalities in their brain, specifically in areas associated with emotional empathy, but whatever the ultimate cause, the result is that they are unable to respond meaningfully and emotionally to others and express care and concern for them. That's a big hurdle to truly loving someone.

They have trouble seeing themselves clearly, so they also can't see others clearly. The best they can do is experience other people as mere extensions of themselves. They don't see them as separate individuals who have their own needs, desires, and feelings. They also tend to overestimate their own capacity for emotional empathy, and their rigidly constructed defenses distort their perceptions of the interactions they have with other people.

These defenses cause the narcissist to use techniques like bragging and withdrawal to keep others at a distance and prevent any appearance of vulnerability. They will also project the negative parts of themselves onto the people around them, and they use denial, entitlement, and tools of narcissistic abuse to ward off the shame they feel inside. These tools include things like gaslighting, lying, shaming, blaming, and even callously insulting others or attempting to destroy them, all in the name of sustaining their carefully crafted illusion of perfection.

Although the narcissist uses these tactics to defend themselves, the truth is that they impair their ability to see or even entertain someone else's reality. That means they can't see that another person loves them. Though they have a degree of emotional intelligence, they use that for manipulation and exploitation rather than developing a genuine understanding of other people's realities. They are, in effect, desensitized to the pain they inflict on those they supposedly love.

How is Love Measured?

It's hard to get inside someone's heart and know if they are really feeling love, but we can examine what love looks like. We can examine what makes people feel like they are loved. Here are some common features that make healthy people feel as if someone loves them:

- **Words of affirmation**—when you affirm that someone is kind, loving, intelligent, warm, giving, and beautiful, these are words of affirmation, and when someone tells you those kinds of things, you tend to believe they love you. This also involves giving you emotional and moral support as you face life's challenges and expressing their feelings for you—actually saying, "I love you;"
- **Quality time**—quality time means spending time getting to know and understand someone in your life, and when someone takes that time, you tend to feel loved. This also involves showing interest in your affairs. Someone who spends quality time with you wants to know what's going on in your life;
- **Gift-giving**—when someone feels strongly enough about you to give you the things you need or want, it tells you they love you;
- **Acts of service**—when someone does things for you that you might have difficulty doing for

yourself, it's an act of love. It might be something as simple as fixing your car for you or running an errand when you don't have time, but these acts signal that they love you;
- **Physical touch**—when someone wants to touch you, you feel desired, and when those physical touches are tender, you feel loved.
- **Tolerates flaws and demands**—when someone is willing to put up with your idiosyncrasies, you typically feel loved and accepted.

These are how healthy people measure love, but it's different for the narcissist. For the narcissist, love is measured with admiration, adoration, and compliance. They need you to prop them up, and if you do so, they feel loved. The problem is in how they feel love—it is that feeling of being on top of the world, when you're being recognized for being so great. They don't necessarily want to have to do what it takes to earn that recognition; they just want to receive it because it bolsters their fragile self-esteem. For the narcissist, love is sacrificial adoration—that is, you would sacrifice yourself in adoration of them, and you would do so without having any kind of real intimacy with them.

Conclusion

The above list of things that make healthy people feel loved are often hard for narcissists to fulfill. Those kinds of expressions of love are frightening for the narcissist because it means you will be getting very close to them. You might see the truth about them, and that is something they fear the most. It makes them dismissive, remote, or even aggressive, and these are not the qualities that most people associate with someone who loves them.

That doesn't mean that narcissists are capable of feeling or even understanding your feelings, but the childhood trauma they often experienced means that they have trouble expressing those feelings or acting out of that understanding for your feelings. There are ways to help them express their love and ways that you can help them understand your feelings and motivate them to show what they feel. But you do have to realize that their love is conditional, and navigating that reality in a relationship with a narcissist requires a lot of patience, strong boundaries, and large amounts of self-care.

In short, asking whether or not a narcissist can love you might be the wrong question to ask. The better question might be: do *you* feel loved? Do you feel valued, are your needs being met, and do you feel like they care about you? If not, is there something you can do to change that so you do feel those things and your needs are being met. This requires you to take a closer look at what you want for your life. There are ways to manage your relationship with a narcissist so you can feel loved by them, but it will take a strong commitment on your part. In the end, you may still end up leaving, but at least you will know you tried your best. In the next chapter, I'll have some final words for you to consider.

Final Words

I know the pain, confusion, and frustration that characterizes a relationship with a narcissist. I have lived that reality, and I made the decision to leave. But I also know that many people cannot or will not make that same decision, and that's why I wanted to write this set of books.

They say that you must understand "the nature of the beast," and this first book in a set of two has provided you with an understanding of the narcissist you love. Even though I chose to leave the narcissist in my life, my experience left me feeling so confused and lost that I needed to understand what had happened and why. I needed to know what was motivating his behavior. Dealing with any kind of mental disorder requires compassionate understanding, even if you don't stay in the relationship.

If you can't leave the narcissist in your life because you still love them, they're one of your children or a parent, or they're a coworker and you don't want to leave your job, you need to understand them. When you know what is going on in their mind and how they see the world, you can develop compassion for their distorted worldview. You can see the effects of their trauma, and you can see their humanity.

That doesn't mean, however, that you should allow yourself to suffer from narcissistic abuse. If, after learning about what causes narcissism, you make the decision to stay in the relationship, you'll need to learn proper strategies for protecting yourself from their emotional abuse. That will be the topic of my second book in this set. It will be designed to help you not only protect yourself, but thrive in the relationship.

The most important thing to realize is that no matter who is in your life, you deserve to be respected and to find genuine love. You don't have to tolerate any kind of abuse, and you can make the decision to go no-contact once it gets to be too much. Understanding the narcissist is the first step in deciding what is best for you.

I felt so alone when I went through my experience with my ex-husband, and it is my genuine desire that you know someone is in your corner. I want to help, no matter what you decide to do in your situation. I want to help you understand narcissism and develop strategies that can work for you, so you can find the happiness you truly desire and deserve. You might think you made a mistake, just as I thought, but the only mistake you would make is if you disrespect yourself. You might choose to stay in your relationship, but you don't have to remain emotionally abused.

You've taken the first step toward understanding the trauma and pain that creates a narcissist. The next step is to develop the strategies you need to live a happy, satisfying life. There is a way, and I am happy to be your guide on that journey. Please feel free to contact me anytime. I want to help you in any way that I can because I do understand what you're going through. Here is my Facebook page if you wish to contact me - https://facebook.com/elena.miro.psychotherapy

By sharing my experiences, I hope to help you realize that you are not alone or crazy, and there is hope. My message to you is that you deserve a happy life filled with true love—don't settle for anything less than that.

I hope you've been helped by this book, and I truly would like to hear your feedback. Please take a moment to leave your review. Reviews are incredibly helpful—both for other readers to decide whether the book will be useful to them, and for new authors like myself to get the word out. So your support is very important. I truly appreciate feedback from my readers, and I love to hear success stories. I hope to hear one from you soon!

Thank you!

Love yourself and be brave!

A wonderful life is waiting for you ahead!

Warm regards,

Elena Miro.

Read the next book in this set

WHAT NARCISSISTS NEVER TELL YOU

THE SECRETS FOR LIVING HAPPILY EVEN WITH A NARCISSIST, PSYCHOPATH, OR OTHER TOXIC PERSON IN YOUR LIFE

ELENA MIRO

Image Sources

Intro#1: https://www.pinterest.com/pin/193373377728530106/

Chapter One Image: https://theweirdpeople.com/get-truth-out-narcissist-dealing-with-narcissist/

Chapter Two Image: https://www.yourtango.com/2019326398/narcissist-quotes-about-narcissistic-personality-disorder

Chapter Three Image: https://unsplash.com/photos/6VWTC9sWu8M

Chapter Four Image: https://media.allauthor.com/images/quotes/gif/christopher-lasch-quote-in-an-individualistic-culture-the.gif

Chapter Five Image: https://unsplash.com/s/photos/the-word-me

Chapter Six Image: https://www.yourtango.com/2016296817/inspiring-quotes-for-anyone-who-has-loved-a-narcissist

Chapter Seven Image: http://www.picturequotes.com/if-you-gave-your-inner-genius-as-much-credence-as-your-inner-critic-you-would-be-light-years-ahead-quote-463227

Chapter Eight Image: https://quotesgram.com/img/narcissist-quotes/12862872/

Chapter Nine Image: https://www.pinterest.com/pin/490962796861320282/

Chapter Ten Image: https://www.yourtango.com/2018312830/best-demi-lovato-quotes-song-lyrics-demi-lovato-music

Final Words Image: https://unsplash.com/photos/WQC8HvAU2SY

Sources

Amanda Chan, HuffPost. (2020, December 7). *18 Ways To Spot A Narcissist*. HuffPost. https://www.huffpost.com/entry/signs-of-narcissism_n_5a26cf6de4b069df71fa196b

Ambardar, S. (2019a, November 10). *Narcissistic Personality Disorder: Practice Essentials, Background, Pathophysiology and Etiology*. Medscape. https://emedicine.medscape.com/article/1519417-overview

Ambardar, S. (2019b, November 10). *What is the prevalence of narcissistic personality disorder (NPD) in the US?* Medscape. https://www.medscape.com/answers/1519417-101779/what-is-the-prevalence-of-narcissistic-personality-disorder-npd-in-the-us#:%7E:text=It%20is%20estimated%20that%20NPD,from%20a%20mental%20health%20professional.

Bell, J. (2020, July 1). *The psychology of narcissism explained*. Big Think. https://bigthink.com/mind-brain/what-is-narcissism

Campbell, W. K., & Twenge, J. M. (2013, November 27). *Narcissism Unleashed.* Association for Psychological Science - APS. https://www.psychologicalscience.org/observer/narcissism-unleashed

Cherry, K. (2019, November 26). *The 10 Needs of Neurotic People.* Verywell Mind. https://www.verywellmind.com/horneys-list-of-neurotic-needs-2795949

Corbano, E. (2019, March 27). *21 Shocking Quotes About Narcissists That Will Make You Leave.* LovesAGame.Com - Breakup Recovery For Adults. https://lovesagame.com/quotes-about-narcissists/

Figueira, E. (2017, May 23). *10 Things Narcissists Fear Most – Psych2Go.* Psych2Go. https://psych2go.net/10-things-narcissists-fear/#:%7E:text=Narcissists%20feed%20heavily%20on%20the,lack%20of%20admiration%20from%20others.&text=Admiration%20from%20others%20is%20the,without%20it%20they%20are%20nothing.

Firestone, L. (2019, January 17). *What Really Goes On in the Mind of a Narcissist?* PsychAlive. https://www.psychalive.org/what-really-goes-on-in-the-mind-of-a-narcissist/

Gaba, S. (2019, May 29). *Trauma Bonding, Codependency, and Narcissistic Abuse A codependent person recognizes that relationships have similar patterns.* Psychology Today. https://www.psychologytoday.com/intl/blog/addiction-and-recovery/201905/trauma-bonding-codependency-and-narcissistic-abuse

Goodreads. (n.d.). *Narcissism Quotes (577 quotes).* Retrieved March 15, 2021, from https://www.goodreads.com/quotes/tag/narcissism

Greenberg, E. (2018, February 17). *7 Steps to Changing Your Narcissistic Responses There's a better way to deal with the issues that trigger your rage.* Psychology Today. https://www.psychologytoday.com/us/blog/understanding-narcissism/201802/7-steps-changing-your-narcissistic-responses

Grubner, B. (2017). Narcissism in cultural theory: Perspectives on Christopher Lasch, Richard Sennett, and Robert Pfaller. *Frontiers of Narrative Studies, 3*(1), 50–70. https://doi.org/10.1515/fns-2017-0004

Kim, J. (2019, June 12). *The Three Subtypes of Narcissistic Personality Disorder The definition and range of this often misunderstood condition are complex.* Psychology Today. https://www.psychologytoday.com/intl/blog/culture-shrink/201906/the-three-subtypes-narcissistic-personality-disorder

Lancer, D. (2018, July 31). *Can You Tell Whether a Narcissist Really Loves You? Even when they say "I love you," can you believe it?* Psychology Today. https://www.psychologytoday.com/us/blog/toxic-relationships/201807/can-you-tell-whether-narcissist-really-loves-you

Lasch, C. (1979). *Culture of Narcissism: American Life in an Age of Diminishing Expectations by Christopher Lasch (15-Jan-1979) Hardcover* (2nd prt. ed.). W.W. Norton.

LT Learning Theories. (2020, March 5). *Narcissism (Kernberg).* Learning Theories. https://www.learning-theories.com/narcissism-kernberg.html

MacDonald, P. (2014). Narcissism in the modern world. *Psychodynamic Practice, 20*(2), 144–153. https://doi.org/10.1080/14753634.2014.894225

Mayo Clinic. (2017, November 18). *Narcissistic personality disorder - Symptoms and causes.* https://www.mayoclinic.org/diseases-conditions/narcissistic-personality-disorder/symptoms-causes/syc-20366662#:%7E:text=Narcissistic%20personality%20disorder%20%E2%80%94%20one%20of,lack%20of%20empathy%20for%20others.

Miller, K. (2020, October 22). *Avoid All 6 Types of Narcissists—but Mental-Health Pros Say One Type Is Especially Damaging.* Well+Good. https://www.wellandgood.com/types-of-narcissists/

Milstead, K. (2020, July 29). *5 Personality Traits That Attract Narcissists & Abusers.* YourTango. https://www.yourtango.com/2018311194/5-personality-traits-attract-narcissists-relationships

Mosquera, D., & Gonzalez, A. (2020, September 6). *Narcissism as a consequence of trauma and early experiences.* ESTD. http://estd.org/narcissism-consequence-trauma-and-early-experiences#:%7E:text=The%20development%20of%20narcissistic%20traits,the%20child%20as%20they%20are.

NPR. (2012, December 4). *The Challenges Of Treating Personality Disorders.* https://choice.npr.org/index.html?origin=https://www.npr.org/2012/12/04/166503627/the-challenges-posed-by-personality-disorders

NPR Talk of the Nation. (2012, December 4). *The Challenges Of Treating Personality Disorders.* NPR.Org. https://www.npr.org/2012/12/04/166503627/the-challenges-posed-by-personality-disorders

Pangilinan, J. (2021, February 22). *41 Quotes About Narcissists to help you Deal With This Selfish Personality Disorder*. Happier Human. https://www.happierhuman.com/narcissist-quotes/

Quora. (n.d.-a). *Are narcissists able to genuinely love ever?* Retrieved March 18, 2021, from https://www.quora.com/Are-narcissists-able-to-genuinely-love-ever

Quora. (n.d.-b). *Can a narcissist ever love someone?* Retrieved March 18, 2021, from https://www.quora.com/search?q=can%20a%20narcissist%20ever%20love%20someone

Quora. (n.d.-c). *How does a narcissist think and feel inside?* Retrieved March 16, 2021, from https://www.quora.com/How-does-a-narcissist-think-and-feel-inside

Quora. (n.d.-d). *How many levels or kinds of narcissists are there? - Quora*. Retrieved March 15, 2021, from https://www.quora.com/How-many-levels-or-kinds-of-narcissists-are-there

Quora. (n.d.-e). *What are the biggest lessons you have learned in the corporate world? - Quora.* Retrieved March 15, 2021, from https://www.quora.com/What-are-the-biggest-lessons-you-have-learned-in-the-corporate-world

Quora. (n.d.-f). *What do narcissists feel inside? - Quora.* Retrieved March 15, 2021, from https://www.quora.com/What-do-narcissists-feel-inside

Quora. (n.d.-g). *What Do Narcissists Hate and Fear the Most?* Retrieved March 16, 2021, from https://www.quora.com/What-do-narcissists-hate-and-fear-the-most

Quora. (n.d.-h). *What do narcissists say about loving others?* Retrieved March 18, 2021, from https://www.quora.com/search?q=what%20do%20narcissists%20say%20about%20loving%20others

Quora. (n.d.-i). *What is narcissism? - NEW - Quora.* Retrieved March 15, 2021, from https://www.quora.com/q/new/What-is-narcissism

Quora. (n.d.-j). *What makes someone a narcissist? - Quora*. Retrieved March 15, 2021, from https://www.quora.com/What-makes-someone-a-narcissist

Quora. (n.d.-k). *When did you realize the person in your life was a narcissist? - Quora*. Retrieved March 15, 2021, from https://www.quora.com/When-did-you-realize-the-person-in-your-life-was-a-narcissist

Quora. (n.d.-l). *Why are people becoming so narcissistic now than ever? - Quora*. Retrieved March 15, 2021, from https://www.quora.com/Why-are-people-becoming-so-narcissistic-now-than-ever

Quora. (n.d.-m). *Why are there so many narcissists? - Quora*. Retrieved March 15, 2021, from https://www.quora.com/Why-are-there-so-many-narcissists

Sheenie Ambardar, M. D., & Bienenfeld, D. (2019, November 10). *What is the prevalence of narcissistic personality disorder (NPD) in the US?* Medscape. https://www.medscape.com/answers/1519417-101779/what-is-the-prevalence-of-narcissistic-personality-disorder-npd-in-the-us#:%7E:text=It%20is%20estimated%20that%20NPD,from%20a%20mental%20health%20professional.

Soeiro, L. (2019, April 22). *4 Types of Narcissist, and How to Spot Each One Not every narcissistic personality functions exactly the same way.* Psychology Today. https://www.psychologytoday.com/us/blog/i-hear-you/201904/4-types-narcissist-and-how-spot-each-one

The Mend Project. (2020, December 1). *The Most Toxic Form of Emotional Abuse: Withholding.* https://themendproject.com/emotional-abuse-withholding/

Vater, A., Moritz, S., & Roepke, S. (2018). Correction: Does a narcissism epidemic exist in modern western societies? Comparing narcissism and self-esteem in East and West Germany. *PLOS ONE*, *13*(5), e0198386. https://doi.org/10.1371/journal.pone.0198386

Waters, D. (2018, March 13). *Why Men Are More Narcissistic (And How to Get It in Check)*. Observer. https://observer.com/2018/03/studies-show-men-are-more-narcissistic-heres-why/

Zajenkowski, M., Maciantowicz, O., Szymaniak, K., & Urban, P. ł. (2018). Vulnerable and Grandiose Narcissism Are Differentially Associated With Ability and Trait Emotional Intelligence. *Frontiers in Psychology*, *9*, 1–8. https://doi.org/10.3389/fpsyg.2018.01606

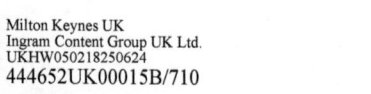